CULTIVATING
A DAILY MEDITATION

---

*Selections from a discourse on
Buddhist view, meditation and action*

by

Tenzin Gyatso
His Holiness the XIVth Dalai Lama

LIBRARY OF TIBETAN WORKS AND ARCHIVES

Line illustrations: Kelsang Wangmo

ISBN: 81-85102-79-1

Published by the Library of Tibetan Works and Archives,
Dharamsala, and printed at Indraprastha Press (CBT),
4 Bahadur Shah Zafar Marg, New Delhi-110002.

Contents

Publisher's Preface

During April of 1985 and then again in October of 1986, His Holiness the Dalai Lama delivered a series of discourses on Buddhist view, meditation and action.

The audience was exclusively Indian. The event had been requested and organized by an interested group from New Delhi. A number of the members had known His Holiness for several years, and the setting was traditional yet informal. The discourse and ensuing discussions were recorded at the time, and a later examination of the materials revealed the makings of an interesting volume on the nature of the Buddhist perspective. We felt that it may be useful to prepare an edited text of the encounter for the international reading public.

In his discourse His Holiness touches upon all the essential points of the Buddhadharma and provides a clear and simple map to how we can cultivate a daily practice of meditation. He also goes into depth on how we should proceed in the effort to generate both the heart of compassion and the expansive view of emptiness, the Great Void, during our daily life. In addition, the question and answer sessions that follow each talk make for both inspirational and informative reading; being open discussions, they often lead to issues that arise in the course of a lay person's practice.

In Chapter Three His Holiness makes use of two brief meditational texts. The first of these is *Eight Verses for Training the Mind*, a twelfth century work of the Kadampa contemplative tradition. At the Library of Tibetan Works and Archives we had earlier published a more extensive commentary to this short work as given by His Holiness in a discourse some years ago, in a collection entitled *Four Essential Buddhist Commentaries*. This may also be useful to those interested in pursuing the study of the *Eight Verses* more deeply.

The other text that His Holiness utilizes is a brief work he composed two decades ago at the request of the late Mr. John Blofeld. Entitled *A Tantric Meditation Simplified for Beginners*, we have included it as an Appendix. The work is a meditation manual, intended to be used by practitioners as the basis of a meditation session. Thus it begins with the usual procedures of preparing the place of meditation, arranging the altar, sitting on one's cushion and correcting motivation, taking refuge and generating the mind of enlightenment, creating the visualization to be used in the meditation, radiating lights, reciting the mantras, and so forth.

A translation of this piece had been made by Ven. Tenzin Khedup in coordination with Mr. John Blofeld and was originally published as a booklet by the Private Office in 1971. Readers may benefit from glancing through it (as reprinted in the Appendix) a few times before venturing into Chapter Three. His Holiness first introduces this text in Chapter Three and then comes back to it in each of the ensuing chapters, expanding upon traditional Buddhist meditations that can be incorporated into the practice.

In a sense His Holiness' discourse can be characterized as being principally a commentary on how one should proceed in order to cultivate a daily tantric meditational practice. We have titled the book accordingly. The visualization used as the basis of the contemplation is that of Buddha and the four great Bodhisattvas: Avalokiteshvara, Manjushri, Vajrapani, and the female bodhisattva Arya Tara. His Holiness explains the symbolic significance of these figures, various ways of meditating upon them, and the recitation of their mantras. The other subjects that he discusses can be regarded as providing the context of the practice.

His Holiness opened his discourse by saying, "This is the first time that I have spoken about the Buddhadharma to such a large Indian audience. Because you are Indians, the subject that I am going to speak about belongs to you and not to me."

He continued, "The Tibetans had a different religion when Buddhism first started to make itself known in the Land of Snows many centuries ago. I think that we were intelligent and open enough to compare the two, our older religion with Buddhism; and in the end the majority of Tibetans adopted Buddhism. Thus for more than a thousand years now Buddhism has been preserved in our country. It brought great benefits to us as a people, both to individual Tibetan practitioners and also to our collective civilization."

Two days later, at the beginning of the mid-afternoon session His Holiness commented, "Many of my foreign friends have said to me that the greatest quality of the Tibetans is that they are so strongly characterized by the good heart, a warm, clear and friendly spirit. This is something that I believe we get from our practice of Buddhism, one of the most precious jewels of India. It gives us an inner joy and strength that we would not otherwise have."

"In particular it has been of immeasurable benefit to us over the last three decades when we have had to witness the loss of our country, the deaths of many loved ones and have had to live as refugees in a foreign land. The kindness of India in receiving us is something that we as a people will never forget; nor have we forgotten the spiritual link that we have with you through Buddhism. Therefore whenever Indian friends want to come and discuss the Dharma with me, I am especially delighted."

Just as His Holiness is pleased to speak of the holy Dharma with an Indian audience, descendants of the civilization that inspired and sustained the original Buddhist masters, the Library of Tibetan Works and Archives is also deeply indebted to India for the kindness it has shown us over the years. We were excited at the prospect of publishing the substance of the discussions.

With this in mind, the Library of Tibetan Works and Archives approached Prof. Dexter Roberts of the University of Montana, an old friend of our institution, with the request to prepare the work for publication.

Prof. Roberts kindly agreed, and thus the fundamental structure of the text emerged. The manuscript was then edited and prepared for publication by Jeremy Russell and Glenn H. Mullin, two honorary members of LTWA's Research and Translation Bureau. I would like to thank them for their efforts.

I would like to offer special thanks to Mr. Rajiv Mehrotra, the New Delhi filmmaker who originally requested and organized the discourse, as well as later providing us with great encouragement and support in the preparation of the work for publication.

Thanks must also go to the translator, Ven. Thupten Jinpa; to Anila Ursula, who transcribed the audio recordings of the event; to Namgyal Dolma and Tsering Norzom, who did much of the computer work in the editing process; and to Jim Woolsey and Norbu Chophel who set the text on our desktop publishing system.

I would like to comment that the policy of our editors has been simply to sharpen the English expression of His Holiness, as is required in publishing a spoken transcript. His Holiness taught large parts directly in English; at other times he spoke through his translator. We took the editorial liberty of harmonizing the styles. But we took great pains to ensure that the meaning is retained in its entirety and not to interfere with the flavour or directness of His Holiness' thoughts and language format. Basic structural sequence and development of ideas is also carefully maintained.

A number of His Holiness the Dalai Lama's discussions with the Indian *intelligencia* have been published in the past. The content of many of these has appeared as magazine and journal articles or in related books on Tibet and the Tibetans. Indeed, His Holiness usually speaks to or with Indian friends several times a day, often addressing Indian conferences, universities and so forth.

In addition, large numbers of Indians come to many of his public discourses, especially those from the Himalayan areas. But usually these constitute a small fraction of the audience, being far outnumbered by the Tibetans themselves. As a result, His Holiness has to direct much of what he is saying at the majority, the non-Indians.

The audience in the October 1986 discourse was from a modern, urban background. Consequently His Holiness spoke within something of a different framework. The meetings produced remarkable results, and LTWA is delighted to be able to bring them to the wider audience made possible through the powers invoked by the printed word.

The picture that emerges from the totality of His Holiness' exposition is that Buddhism, in spite of its being labelled a religion, is mainly a way of life programmed to ensure that we bring some happiness, peace, meaning and purpose into our lives and that we learn to live in harmony with the environment.

The tantric meditation that His Holiness suggests has this as its aim. By always keeping the five enlightenment figures in the sphere of our mindfulness drawing inspiration from the five qualities that they symbolize—control, compassion, wisdom, energy and beneficial activity—we find that our lives become more pervaded by the experience of happiness, peace, meaning and purpose.

Gyatsho Tshering
Director,
Library of Tibetan Works and Archives,
Dharamsala H.P. India
December 25, 1990

Addendum to Publisher's Preface

We are happy to bring out this revised edition of *Cultivating a Daily Meditation* wherein we have corrected the typographical errors, recomposed the type settings and provided a new cover. This title has been printed three times in the past and has benefited many people interested in cultivate a daily practice of meditation.

Like in the previous editions, we have retained the original structure and thoughts of His Holiness' teachings so as to maintain its clarity and simplicity.

We would like to thank Ms. Linda Roman and Ms. Tashi Yangzom for rendering necessary assistance in bringing out this edition.

Publication Department
Library of Tibetan Works and Archives
Dharamsala, H.P. India

July 9, 2004

Foreword

It is said that Buddhism disappeared from India because it was injudiciously liberal. Buddhism in its homeland finally went the way of all dependent things and progressively became so Hinduised that it lost all reason for a separate existence. The Buddha came to be recognised as the ninth in a series of ten incarnations of Vishnu ascending from the theriomorphic (animal form) to the fully anthromorphic (human form) manifestation. Hinduism has been comfortable with the notion of reincarnation, a concept particularly geared to the social role of Vishnu. Whenever the Dharma is in danger Vishnu departs from his heaven, Vaikuntha, and incarnates himself in an earthly form to restore the good order. That His Holiness the Dalai Lama is regarded as a Bodhisattva, are incarnation of the compassionate Avalokiteshvara form of the Buddhas, in this time of churning and seeming chaos, gives him a unique position in India.

During the more than three decades of his exile in India, His Holiness and the Indian people have had a very special relationship. In this land of a multitude of religions and God-men of every hue, His Holiness is universally revered as a spiritual master of profound wisdom, compassion and insight. He is sought out by all kinds of people, from the humble villager to the university student; from the successful businessman to the activist social worker; the civil servant and the politician, who even if he doesn't stand up for Tibet's political cause seeks the blessings of this man of God. He is in demand at conferences, inaugurations, interfaith congregations, and for unceasing private audiences. India never tires of His Holiness.

In turn, His Holiness has looked to India as his 'spiritual home', that gave Tibet its Buddhism more than a thousand years ago and today is host to more than a hundred thousand of its exiles, amongst and through whom it helps keep that very tradition alive. For India, the Dalai Lama is helping to bring Buddhism back to the land of the Buddha's birth. India, as the West does not always appreciate, long ceased to be a Buddhist country. Buddhism, never a missionary religion, is today carried on his gentle smiling face that even as he reaches out with a serious and vital message is the compelling reminder that the journey can be a joyous one.

The Dalai Lama responded to a request for a set of teachings on Buddhism that could lead to the cultivation of a daily practice. A small group of fifteen—that was urban, educated and exclusively Indian, many of whom describe themselves as Hindu/Buddhists— came together and travelled to Dharamsala by road from Delhi through the violence in Punjab, then at one of its many peaks, for three days of discourses. This went down so well with both the Indians and His Holiness, that another meeting was organised in New Delhi the next October, for a larger group of about seventy-five. This book is an edited transcript of the two events.

No one who has ever heard His Holiness speak will think it at all possible to capture in print the enormous impact of his personality and the many levels at which he communicates. Though much of the formal teachings were in Tibetan with an interpreter translating, inevitably in formal English, His Holiness frequently broke into infectious laughter and his own English to establish a more direct and immediate rapport with his audience. He touched people in powerful ways that frequently evoked emotions and insights that we were only dimly aware off. It was a finely balanced mixture of the transcendental and the every day, of *sutra and tantra* that recommended personal contemplation and altruistic action. He constantly surprised, questioned and overturned old habits, shifting entrenched certainties. He never hesitated to admit 'I don't know!' to the imponderable questions put to him. He carried and shared his erudition and insights with a gentle, easy and comforting grace.

No amount of reading can substitute for the impact and power of a shared experience with a Master. While the discourses touched upon all the essential points of the Dharma, they were aimed at providing a foundation for a daily meditation practice evolved out of the Mahayana tantric tradition. As a rule this depends largely on the oral transmission in an unbroken lineage through a living person in the form of a *Guru*.

In the more advanced meditation practices it also requires an initiation into the techniques through an empowerment ceremony that makes the practitioners mental continuum receptive to the intricate meditative techniques. An expert guide can then lead him through the successive stages of the path. The meditations suggested here were evolved by His Holiness so as not requiring a formal initiation or empowerment, but rather to sow the seeds for it amongst those who were so interested and motivated. That it proved an inspiring and gratifying practice has been demonstrated by the many in the group who went on to receive a formal initiation and took the formal *bodhichitta* vows later, though this was not the assumption of the teachings.

The tantric tradition has remained largely suspect in the popular Hindu perception. It is uncertain whether this is merely a consequence of the condemnation of tantra by virtually all early Western writers on the subject and their impact on the Indians during British colonialism or, as is more likely, Hinduism itself, as it evolved under the impact of foreign invasions and its reforms, misunderstood the sexual element as dominating the entire system of tantra.

While it is true that one of the basic human drives that the tantric system draws upon is desire, it is not limited too or ruled exclusively by the desire of sexuality. According to Buddhism every human being wants happiness and does not want suffering. He has the potential to achieve this. The Buddhist tantra tells us that this remarkable transformation is not only possible but can be achieved very quickly if we draw upon all aspects of our energy, in particular the energy of our desires. Desire, if skillfully used, can be our most valuable resource because it is the most powerful of our drives. We need to develop the ability to use it effectively for our transformation to become fulfilled, happy human beings. What distinguishes Buddhist tantric practice from the evil, manipulative tantric practitioner in pursuit of 'unholy' pleasure whom the Hindu tradition so deeply suspects and fears, is the goal to which desire is disciplined and directed.

His Holiness has ever emphasised altruism as the very basis and internal structure of our practice and the need to direct whatever activities we do towards its increase. We need to thoroughly suffuse our minds with it and use words and writings as a means of reminding ourselves of the goals of our training. This forms the essence of one of the texts used by His Holiness, *Eight Verses Of Training The Mind.*

No words of gratitude are enough to His Holiness for having given us of himself and the teachings, and for permission to print and make these available to a larger audience. It is in our striving that we can prove worthy of this.

My thanks, on behalf of all of us that were privileged to be present at the discourses, go first to Ven. Thupten Jinpa for a splendid job as interpreter and for giving us of his time so patiently even after the teachings; and to Mr. Tenzin Geyche of The Private Office of His Holiness, and Mr. Tashi Wangdi of the Bureau in Delhi, for helping with organising the event. Mr. Gyatsho Tshering, Director of the Library of Tibetan Works and Archives, who has brought this book together and orchestrated the efforts of so many people to make it possible, also deserves our sincere appreciation.

Rajiv Mehrotra
New Delhi, India
10th January 1991

1

Attitude and Activity

Buddha Shakyamuni

The Character of Tibetan Buddhism

There are two ways to teach the Buddhadharma. The teacher can speak as guru to disciples, and in some cases there can be pujas, the making of material and mental offerings to show respect and strengthen devotion before the teachings; or the discussion can be completely informal, not as between guru and disciples.

We will follow the latter of the two ways. I will not use any particular text but will simply explain the essential teachings of the Buddha. Everybody should feel free to ask questions.

I think it is important that you get some basic idea about the Buddhadharma as it was preserved in Tibet, for it still is a living tradition and not only a continuation of oral transmissions. There are people in our small refugee community who have had extraordinary experiences through their own practice. Our tradition is very much alive.

Although, as I said earlier, this is to be an informal discussion, as a Buddhist monk I would like to recite one verse in praise of Gautama Buddha:

> Homage to that perfect Buddha,
> The supreme philosopher,
> Who taught us dependent arising
> Free of destruction and creation,
> Without annihilation and permanence,
> With no coming and no going,
> Neither unity nor plurality,
> The quietening of fabrications,
> The ultimate beatitude!

As you probably know, there are two major schools of Buddhism: Mahayana, which translates as the Greater Vehicle and Hinayana, the Lesser Vehicle.

The system of the Lesser Vehicle was propounded by Buddha Shakyamuni in public teachings. The teachings of the Greater Vehicle were given to groups of people who were already disciples. The latter teachings explain not only techniques for training the mind but also Tantrayana, or techniques for working with vital energies and centers of the body.

Buddhism as preserved and practised by individuals in Tibet for the past many centuries is complete, comprising all three of these levels of teachings.

Take, for example, my own practice. I have adopted bhikshu (monastic) vows according to the *The Sutra on Monastic Discipline*, or the essence of the Lesser Vehicle teachings, in which are included rules binding upon members of the monastic community. My daily life and conduct are based on its teachings; I live as a monk. In our tradition, fully ordained monks observe 273 rules. We have to keep them. Moreover, every day I practise calm abiding (*shamatha, zhi gnas*) and special insight (*vipashyana, lhag mthong*) meditations, which are also teachings of the Lesser Vehicle.

Yet my main daily practice, development of the mind of enlightenment (*bodhichitta, byang chub sems*) based upon compassion (*karuna, snying rje*) and love (*maitri, byams pa*), is from the teachings of the Greater Vehicle. And I practise the six perfections (*paramitas, phar phyin*) of generosity, discipline, patience, vigor, meditation, and wisdom as much as I can. These are teachings of the Greater Vehicle. In addition, I also practise deity yoga with mandalas. This practice is from the Tantrayana teachings. Thus, in Tibet one could practise the essence of these three doctrines simultaneously. This is the unique feature of Tibetan Buddhism, its great breadth of techniques.

To begin nevertheless with a simple approach, we can say that all the teachings of Buddha Shakyamuni can be divided into two categories: conduct and view.

The conduct which Buddha taught is non-violence (*ahimsa, tshe med zhi ba'i lam*), not to harm. Not harming others also includes benefiting them and working for their welfare. Most major world religions teach non-violence. They teach us to be warm-hearted, have a good motivation, good character. In their aim of benefiting all humanity, the major world religions agree.

To accomplish this end, however, different philosophies have arisen, since there exist human beings of many different dispositions. For certain people, certain philosophies are more suitable and effective than others. Therefore, people of different dispositions and interests can engage in the practice of those systems that suit them best.

Irrespective of these different philosophies, the most important point is to have a tamed and disciplined mind and a warm heart. With this perspective, consider two different philosophies and approaches to our spiritual situation. Some religions teach God as a creator, with us as the created. Finally, things depend on God and if we act according to the wishes of God, we shall achieve permanent happiness. The person is nothing and the creator is all-important. If one explains to certain people that everything is in the hands of the Creator, and therefore they should do nothing against his wishes, they act accordingly. It gives them mental satisfaction and moral stability.

Other people approach religious philosophy with scepticism. They rely upon interdependence. If it is explained to them that everything is not in the hands of an almighty creator but in their own hands, they too gain mental satisfaction and moral stability.

This is the Buddhist approach. Although Buddhists can say that if someone harms others he acts against the wishes of the Buddha, this is not the significance of the Buddha's teachings. Buddha taught that the sufferings we do not wish for and the happiness we desire and cherish are all the products of causes and that we control our whole destiny.

In Buddhism, there is no creator. The ultimate creator is one's own mind. This mind is intrinsically pure, and with a positive motivation, our verbal and physical actions can become positive and can produce wholesome results, results that are pleasant and beneficial.

On the other hand when the mind remains coarse, then we commit harsh verbal and physical actions, which by nature harm or hurt others, and the result is unpleasant and painful. One cannot blame others for one's own suffering. One can only blame oneself. The responsibility for it lies on one's own shoulders.

Thus Buddhists believe in self-creation. There is no almighty God or creator.

As the Buddha taught the conduct of non-harming, he taught the view of 'dependent arising' as its complement of wisdom. Dependent arising according to the Buddhist teachings means, as has been suggested, that the happiness which we cherish is the consequence of a cause, and in the same way the suffering which we do not desire is also the consequence of a cause. Therefore we should seek to cultivate the cause of happiness and abandon the cause of suffering.

Dependent arising is explained in detail in the twelve links, the first of which is ignorance and the last death.

The links are explained as a cycle. It is not that we start with ignorance and end with death, thus completing the whole cycle and finishing existence, but rather that the links are different moments of ignorance, and each instance of ignorance has its own action, which in turn gives rise to rebirth. This is an endless cycle. It must be emphasized again that dependent arising explains the happiness and suffering which we are experiencing as the products of causes.

As the Buddha explained in the sutras, specific actions will have specific results, and all effects or fruits are products of one's own actions and causes. Apart from that there is no creator. Nor is there a 'self' with inherent existence and independence of this cause and effect process.

Buddha taught two groups of cause and effect. One is the group of cause and effect of delusions. For example, if the cause is negative

negative thought, the result is suffering. The other is the group of cause and effect of positive actions, for example, if the cause is positive, the result is happiness.

This teaching is expressed in the Four Noble Truths with which the Buddha first turned the wheel of Dharma. The first truth is the truth of suffering, which is divided into three types of suffering. First there is the suffering of suffering, the mental and physical pain which is experienced by human beings, animals, and so forth. Then there is the suffering of change. This refers to the suffering of, for example, hunger and thirst. We eat and drink to overcome this suffering, but if we go on eating and drinking, we create other problems.

The suffering of change is experienced especially in the so-called developed countries. When people there get something new, they feel happy. They have a new camera, a new television set, a new car, and for a moment they are very happy. Soon, however, their happiness starts to diminish as the new article begins to give worries. They throw it away and want another one. They get it, then again the same things happen: initially great happiness and satisfaction, but soon irritation. This is what we mean by the suffering of change.

The third type of suffering is that of conditioning. The main cause of this kind of suffering is our psychophysical aggregates which are a product of our own contaminated actions and delusions. These are the three types of suffering included in the First Noble Truth, the truth of suffering.

Nirvana, or liberation, is release from our suffering. Release from the first two categories alone, however, is not what is meant by nirvana.

We can say when we are sitting here and feeling comfortable that we are free of the first suffering, the suffering of suffering. But we are still potentially afflicted by the second type, that of change.

There are people who, through the force of their mental quiescence, insight and meditation, are able to go beyond the experience of these gross types of suffering and happiness, and remain in a neutral state of mind. They are free from the first two kinds of suffering. But only when these persons are also free from the third type of suffering, that of their conditioned aggregates produced by contaminated actions and delusions, have they achieved nirvana.

In order to find release from suffering, we must investigate its source more closely. This investigation relates to the Second Noble Truth, that of the cause of suffering.

There are two types of causes. One is our own physical and verbal actions, and the other is the delusions of our minds.

For example, if at this moment as I talk to you I use nice words and gentle physical actions, I create a pleasant atmosphere. On the other hand, if I use harsh words and rough physical actions, like beating, I create an unpleasant atmosphere as the immediate result of that action.

While a person is engaged in an action either physically or verbally, he leaves an imprint on his own consciousness. The consciousness on which the person implants that imprint is called the temporary basis of the imprint. The person or self to whom this consciousness belongs is called the permanent basis of the imprint.

Because of the imprint which the action of that person has left on his consciousness, he is bound to experience the consequences of his actions, irrespective of the length of time that elapses. This explains the experience of suffering, which we do not desire, and its cause.

The Third Noble Truth is the truth of the cessation of suffering.

Nirvana, the state in which one is permanently freed from suffering, can be achieved in this lifetime. The means by which we do this is the path to the cessation of suffering, the Fourth Noble Truth.

The basis on which we have to free ourselves from suffering is consciousness, the mind. The truth of the path to cessation involves the cultivation of a very refined state of mind, one endowed with a special quality of wisdom.

To free our minds from suffering and the stains of it, we must understand what is meant by the wisdom of emptiness, or that consciousness which eliminates mental delusions and realizes the nature of reality. Because the understanding of emptiness is very important, there are many different explanations of it. For example, there are the four major schools of Indian Buddhist thought, and the others derived from them.

The Nature of the Mind

Buddhist texts say that the criterion for positing something as existent or non-existent is whether it is perceived by valid cognition or not. Something which is perceived by valid cognition is existent and something which is not perceived by valid cognition is non-existent.

In the category of existent objects are two type of phenomenon: firstly, temporary or occasional phenomena, which are sometimes there and sometimes not; and secondly, permanent phenomena, which are always there, such as space.

The fact that some phenomena occasionally exist shows that they depend on causes and conditions, and therefore they are called products. The phenomena which do not depend on causes and conditions exist permanently or eternally, and they are called non-products.

There are many different types within the first category of phenomenon. Some of them have the qualities of visibility, like form, shape, colour and so forth, and these are collectively known as form. Other types of phenomenon which are products but do not have the quality of form are known as formless, for example, consciousness or knowledge. Then there is another type of phenomena, which is a mere abstract entity, such as time, self, etc. Thus there are such phenomena as form, consciousnesses, and abstract things, which are neither of these two. Forms include phenomena such as those which are objects of our sensory consciousnesses. This refers to form as perceived by our eye-consciousness, smell perceived by nose-consciousness and similarly sound, touch and taste.

We have two major categories of consciousness: primary consciousnesses, which depend on their respective sense faculties as their immediate conditions; and secondary consciousnesses, or mental attitudes and elements, which have no particular sense faculties of their own, but which always accompany the primary consciousnesses. These are also known as mental factors.

Primary consciousnesses are divided into two: sensory consciousnesses, which depend on sense faculties; and mental consciousnesses.

Fifty-one types of secondary mental attitudes and elements are explained. This includes the five ever-present secondary mental elements: feeling, recognition, mental impulses, decisive attention and contact. These are called "ever-present" because they invariably accompany each primary mental consciousness. Then there are the five discriminating mental factors, eleven generally positive mindset, six root defilements or delusions, twenty secondary delusions and four variable attitudes.

Sensory consciousnesses arise in dependence on three main conditions. Using as an example the eye-consciousness which perceives this book, the fact that the eye-consciousness perceives this book alone and not the table is an exclusive quality of its object of observation.

Followers of the Great Exposition (*Vaibhashika*) School say that consciousnesses arise without any aspect of their object. *A Treasury of Knowledge* explains that it is the physical eye organ, the sense faculty, which sees the object, and not the consciousness by itself.

Other Buddhist schools such as the Followers of Scripture (*Sautrantika*) and the higher schools say that consciousnesses perceive their object through the aspect of the object.

Although there are many different views as to whether external phenomena exist at all apart from consciousness, I shall explain this according to the system which holds that external phenomena do exist apart from consciousness.

This book serves as objective condition, and it has the quality of appearing to the apprehending consciousness by which it is perceived. That this consciousness sees a form and cannot hear a sound is the exclusive quality of its main condition, which is the sense faculty, the eye-organ. The mere convergence of these, the condition of observation which is the object and the main condition which is the sense faculty, does not mean that one will necessarily experience this consciousness. For example, during sleep or when the mind is distracted by something else, we might look at something, but not be aware of it.

This shows that there is another condition apart from the two, and that is the immediately preceding condition. This refers to the previous instant of consciousness, which makes perception possible through experience. The object is there and the eye-organ is there, but if the brain does not function well, then this consciousness cannot function, cannot come into being. This shows that there the brain is an additional factor.

Still the brain alone does not have the power or ability to produce an experience of eye-consciousness, and this shows that there exists still another factor, which is the mental consciousness depending upon the brain.

The ways in which sensory consciousnesses like the eye-consciousness, nose-consciousness, and so forth arise and experience their objects are similar to one another.

Sensory consciousnesses are said to be non-conceptual. When, for example, we look at this book, although we look at it in a general way, there is a certain factor which focuses attention on this one article, this particular piece of material. As explained earlier, when our mind is attracted by a form we are looking at, then even if we hear a sound, we will not register it. We are not aware of it and will not remember it. In the same way, if we are enthralled by a melodious sound, we might see something, but we have no awareness of it, and cannot recollect it later.

This shows that there is a certain factor involved apart from sensory consciousness, and that factor is the mental consciousness.

There are two types of mental consciousness: conceptual and non-conceptual. Non-conceptual mental consciousness is also known as direct perception.

Apart from disagreement between different schools on whether or not there is self-perceiving direct perception, all Buddhist schools accept three direct perceptions: sensory, mental and yogic direct perception. This last is achieved through meditation.

All of the six primary consciousnesses, from visual consciousness to that of the mind, always have the five ever-present mental factors. The other of the fifty-one factors are sometimes present and sometimes absent.

Due to their different functions, consciousnesses are divided into two: valid cognition and invalid cognition.

In order to achieve the desired results, we have to follow valid cognition. There are two types of results of valid cognition: uninterrupted results and interrupted results.

There are three types of invalid cognition: non-perception of the object, mistaken consciousness, and wavering. Non-perception includes the consciousness which is presented with the appearance of the object but cannot register, cannot recognize it. Another type of mistaken consciousness is mere assumption. Mistaken consciousness is the consciousness which distorts its object of perception.

There are three kinds of wavering consciousnesses. One inclines toward the truth, one toward wrong perception, and the third is equally balanced between the two.

There are different levels of invalid cognition. In order to counteract them, there are different stages of transformation of consciousness. At the first stage, one has to counteract the single-pointed mistaken view, and for this we have methods such as lines of reason by which one investigates the nature of a given idea.

After the force of single-pointedness is achieved, there comes the stage of hesitation, and then more subtle hesitation. We overcome those, again by using lines of inquiry.

After that we use reason to gain an inferential understanding of the object. When we have developed familiarity with that object, we reach the stage where the consciousness becomes non-conceptual.

There are three types of wisdom: that arising from listening; that arising from contemplation, and that arising from meditation. There are also numerous ways to sub-divide each of these three wisdoms.

This is just a basic explanation of the nature of consciousnesses. In order to understand the topic in detail, one has first to understand the presentation of the different objects of consciousness, then the agents by which one knows these different objects, and then the way in which the consciousness co-operates with the object.

There are different ways in which consciousnesses engage their objects. Therefore non-conceptual consciousnesses have what is called an appearing object, but no object of conceptualization.

Conceptual thought has what is called the object of conceptualization, as well as a certain type of object called an object of apprehension.

Phenomena are also divided into two categories: affirmative phenomena, and negative phenomena. Relative to these two categories, there are also different kinds of conceptual thought, e.g., those which perceive negative and those which perceive affirmative aspects.

For example, this book is an affirmative phenomenon. Therefore, to perceive this book we have to explicitly negate its opposite factor, non-book.

On the other hand, when we say that this table is devoid of book, here the consciousness is operating in a negative way; it is negating its object of negation, which in this case is book. Such a perception is only possible by means of negating something; it cannot be perceived in an affirmative way.

Negative phenomena are also divided into two: affirming negative phenomena and non-affirming negative phenomena. Generally speaking, they are fifteen types of negative phenomenon, but they are condensed into these two major categories of non-affirming and affirming negative phenomena.

There are four types of affirming negative phenomena: those which suggest other phenomena explicitly; those which suggest other phenomena implicitly; those which suggest other phenomena both explicitly and implicitly; and those which suggest other phenomena by context.

In the last case, when we know that something is one of two possible entities, and when we say that it is not this one, then without saying so, we know that it is the other one.

An example of how we know something implicitly, without expressing it explicitly, is to say that a fat man does not eat during the day, which implies that he eats at night.

An example of a non-affirming statement is, "This Brahmin does not drink alcohol." The statement merely negates the Brahmin's drinking of alcohol, but does not suggest that he drinks anything else.

It is very important to understand these negative phenomena, because emptiness, being a negative phenomenon, can only be explained in terms of a negating approach.

Questions and Answers

Question: You seem to suggest that certain religious practices are appropriate for certain people. How does one really know which practices are appropriate for oneself?

His Holiness: At the beginning you simply experiment with different methods that might be effective. Later, at a higher stage, through dreams or different kinds of unusual experiences, you can investigate in special ways.

What I meant by saying that all major religions have the one aim to make better human beings is simply that they are the same in this respect.

Beyond that, however, there are differences within the various spiritual traditions.

One group, for example, the Christians, believe that human beings can ultimately reach heaven. Other groups, such as Buddhists and some other ancient Indian traditions, believe that human beings can reach nirvana, liberation (*moksha*)

Yet there are different definitions of nirvana even within Buddhism. For example, the Great Exposition (*Vaibhashika*) School of Buddhism, one of the schools of the Lesser Vehicle, asserts that *Mahaparinirvana*, the great stage of final nirvana achieved by an enlightened being at the time of physical death, is not a state which is only free of mental delusions but is also free of the mind itself. For them there exists no continuity of the mind. According to that understanding Buddha Shakyamuni at the present time is only an historical figure. He does not exist any more.

Nagarjuna denied this, asserting that what we call nirvana or liberation is a state where the mind is completely free of all delusions. It does not mean that the mind itself has also ceased. There must be a person who actualizes this state of nirvana. Nagarjuna discusses the status of that person in detail.

Thus even among the systems which agree on the existence of nirvana, there are differences. And even among Buddhists there are differences in the presentation.

If Christians were asked whether there existed a Christian practice by which such a state of nirvana could be achieved, the answer would have to be no. In the same way, if we as Buddhists were asked if there were a Buddhist practice by which we could go to heaven as Christians do, the answer again would have to be no.

In order to achieve the state of nirvana as explained in Buddhism, a complete system of methods has to be practised.

There are many people who are not interested in the practice of that path. For them, some other spiritual tradition may be more appropriate.

Question: Since this path depends so much on reason, wouldn't there be a tendency to dismiss unusual experiences as something illogical, and not to investigate them?

His Holiness: There is such a thing as yogic direct perception. Such experiences are at present hidden from most of us, so we can understand their existence only by inference.

Certain experiences we can infer through our gross levels of mind and others through subtle levels of mind. During sleep, in the dream-state, our consciousness has reached a subtler level than during the waking state, and this provides us with the opportunity to have a glimpse of certain experiences which are not possible during the waking state, when the mind is active on grosser levels.

Because of that, one can actually engage in certain investigations during the dream-state.

In the waking state, one can infer through reasoning that the consciousness by which one knows has the quality of clarity, the potential to know things without any obscurations.

Through reasoning processes we investigate and verify the possibility of unusual experiences; for example, that there exist certain things which one can only understand through unusual methods, such as experiences in dreams.

Question: How do we interpret dreams? Does this require skill, a psychological approach or what?

His Holiness: We are not talking here about dreams generally but for example, of a certain dream that may repeat itself again and again.

The dreams that are important are not the ones we have just after falling asleep, but rather those experienced during the time of dawn. We should investigate dreams repeatedly experienced during dawn.

If one is very serious about this experiment and wants to go further, at a deeper level, one investigates dreams with the assistance of certain yogas employing the subtle bodily energy-winds. Through this practice dreams become clearer and more definite.

Generally, however, dreams are something which one takes to be illusive, without any truth. According to the Middle Way Consequentialists, the highest Buddhist school, all of our experiences of consciousness even during the waking state are said to be mistaken in being dependent on the appearance of the objects. We misperceive our experiences when awake, so in dreams our experiences can be even more mistaken.

Question: Since the risk seems to be one of delusion, what practice is necessary so that one can distinguish between delusion and reality?

His Holiness: When we talk about consciousness during the waking state being deluded, this is according to the ultimate level. On the conventional level, however, valid cognition exists.

Valid cognition is of two types, direct and inferential. Most often we use the latter kind in day-to-day life, questioning our own understanding and asking others about theirs. If we find ourselves as a result of this questioning in a state of indecision, then we must first of all keep calm; there is no use feeling anxious, making oneself nervous. The theory of karma and the realization that the entire worldly existence is of the nature of suffering will help us to keep calm. Then investigate.

Question: How can we distinguish when the mind is misleading us and when it is not? The mind is the tool which we are using for reasoning, and when the mind itself is deluded, what can we do?

His Holiness: This requires an explanation of the two types of correct views: the correct worldly view and the correct view which is beyond the worldly level.

The view which is beyond the worldly level refers to the realization of the nature of phenomena, which means emptiness. The appearance of phenomena as if they had some kind of inherent existence, as if they existed in their own right, is a mistaken perception. Due to the influence of this mistaken perception we grasp at their supposedly true existence. In order to know that our own consciousness, which sees them, is mistaken, it is necessary first to realize that phenomena themselves do not have such an exaggerated nature, that they are not inherently existent, that they lack true existence.

Through the realization of their nature, one can see that the consciousness to which phenomena appear in such a way is also mistaken.

When we experience emotional afflictions like aversion or attachment, the object of our repulsion or desire appears as if it were something solid and independent, which will never change. Once we realize that the object of our attention does not really exist as we see it, this will reduce our afflicted emotions of hatred or desire. At this stage we meditate on emptiness.

Question: Your Holiness, on a somewhat lower spiritual or intellectual level, what kind of real control do we have in the workings of karma?

His Holiness: There are different types of karma, and one of them we accumulate collectively and have to experience collectively. Other types of karma, accumulated individually, have to be experienced individually.

That all of us had the possibility to gather here today is the consequence of karma which we have accumulated collectively. However, this does not mean that all these karmas were collected together at the same place, at the same time.

We have no control over actions or karma which we have accumulated in the past. We have to experience their results, or purify ourselves of them. But we do have control over our own karma in so far as what we shall experience in the future is determined by our own actions of the present time.

Question: I think the dilemma is that if we all carry karmic influences which govern our actions, where does free will operate, simultaneously in co-existence with karmic influences?

His Holiness: As I just said, there is no control over karma that we have accumulated in the past. Those actions have been done, and imprints are left on our consciousness; we have to experience their results. But what we are going to experience in the future is in our own hands, is determined by ourselves. For example, if we commit a crime, as a result we have to face the consequences of that action.

However, there is the possibility of neutralizing past negative karma through practices of spiritual purification. In the same way, positive karma accumulated in the past can be destroyed through forceful negative actions like anger.

It is also possible that one forceful, positive karmic seed can overwhelm another, non-virtuous karma; and that good karma can be saved from destruction through dedication.

Question: What is reborn? Does some identity become part of a larger consciousness, part of which manifests itself again?

His Holiness: The "I".

Another Questioner: But I do not know who that "I" is. If I am born again I do not know that it is I. I do not remember what I was before. Who am I?

His Holiness: The answer to the question of whose continuity of consciousness it is, to whom it belongs, is that it belongs to the being himself.

Whether one can find that self, that I or not is a different question altogether.

If one were to say that for one's previous life to have existed then one has to recollect it, this is not the case. Certain experiences we can remember; others, even of this life, we cannot. But on this basis we cannot say, "that was not me."

There are people who very clearly remember their past lives. Yet ordinary people cannot remember past lives because the level of consciousness during the time of death, the interval state between the previous life and the next life, is most subtle. The subtle level of mind on which those memories are based cannot communicate to our gross conscious mind.

A person who has some experience of utilizing deeper consciousness has a better chance to have clearer memories of past lives.

Question: You said that before we embark on the process to end suffering we must be sure that suffering can be ended, we must have the proof. How can we find this proof?

His Holiness: As the root cause of suffering can be purged or eliminated, suffering itself can be eliminated.

Basically the root cause is the delusions. All these delusions are rooted in the self-grasping attitude.

We must clarify the deluded consciousness which perceives phenomena as inherently existent. Although all Buddhist schools talk of methods for eliminating this mistaken habit of consciousness, the Middle Way system explains that by using logical reasoning for the negation of inherent existence, one can understand emptiness. Through such inquiry one can also establish that the mind can be freed of delusions.

Question: Is liberation an uncovering of an original state, a Buddhanature that is already there?

His Holiness: Buddhist explanations do not say that beings derive from a pure source free of all delusions. Ignorance has no beginning, so suffering has no beginning either, and cyclic existence (*samsara*) has no beginning. When an individual gets to the stage where the mind is free of all delusion, that stage is called liberation.

Buddhanature is the potential which is inherent in the consciousness of everybody and which, when activated by circumstances, can be fully realized. But it is not Buddhahood itself.

Ultimately nirvana has to be explained through the cessation of suffering, or the expansiveness of phenomena, emptiness, into which all these delusions are purified. It is the emptiness of a mind free of all delusions and identical with samsara. There is no difference between samsara and nirvana.

For example, this table is devoid of elephant. The mere absence of that thing, the elephant, is the same as the way in which reality is empty of inherent existence and also devoid of delusion.

The path, the quality of nirvana's being empty of inherent existence, is there within ourselves because our mind too is devoid of inherent existence. Therefore the potential of nirvana is in our mind.

Absence of independent existence is the ultimate nature, emptiness (*shunyata*). Phenomena which exist in dependence on other factors are devoid of independent nature, independent self. Therefore they are empty.

Liberation or nirvana has to be explained from the viewpoint of a being free of mental faults. We cannot talk about nirvana on the basis of a book. Nirvana is explained only on the basis of living beings.

In this modern age Western science has much knowledge about matter, but it seems very limited concerning consciousness. Without deep knowledge of consciousness the usefulness of even full knowledge of matter is questionable. In any case, since for us knowledge is acquired not by sentient beings generally but by human beings, the main purpose of acquiring this knowledge is to benefit humanity.

As that is so, I feel it is very important to have a balanced understanding: knowledge of consciousness through inner experience; and knowledge of matter. If we approach scientific research work one-sidedly and do not take into consideration the fact of internal consciousness, then we automatically neglect the experience of feeling.

For example, powerful, destructive weapons are really a great achievement from the purely materialistic point of view, but when seen in terms of their benefit for mankind, their value is questionable.

I believe that discussion or study of consciousness is not necessarily a religious matter, but important for technical knowledge, human knowledge. In that respect, Eastern philosophy, especially Buddhist philosophy, has something to contribute to the modern world.

2

The Nature of the Path

Avalokiteshvara, Bodhisattva of Compassion

The Two Levels of Truth

Having discussed the basis of phenomena, I shall now explain the stages of the path.

We all innately wish to acquire happiness and to avoid suffering. Buddhism says that we have the natural right to work for these two ends.

The many different categories of happiness and suffering can be divided broadly into physical pleasure and suffering; and mental pleasure and suffering. The latter, the experiences of the mind, are more important than those of the body.

The Buddha said that methods exist by which one can free oneself from mental suffering and achieve bliss. These methods are explained in the third of the Four Noble Truths, the truth of the cessation of suffering.

Cessation, also called liberation or nirvana, is a state of reality free of all faults and delusions.

It is possible to rid the mind of its faults and delusions. To understand how, we must understand the nature of the two truths (as distinct from the Four Noble Truths): ultimate truth and conventional truth.

My explanation of ultimate and conventional truths is based on the Middle Way Consequentialist (*Madhyamika Prasangika*) School.

The four major Buddhist schools, i.e. Middle Way, Mind-Only, Followers of Scripture, and Great Exposition, came into being on the basis of the actual words of the Buddha. Yet these four major schools disagree on the subject under discussion, each validating its presentation by citing the words of the Buddha himself.

How can we say that one is more valid than the others? The Buddha himself suggested the approach to be taken:

> Oh bikkshus and wise men,
> Do not accept my words just because you respect me,
> But analyse them as the goldsmith analyses gold
> And then accept them.

Still more specifically, the Buddhist tenet of the four reliances recommends

> Do not rely on the teacher but on the teachings he gives;
> Do not rely on mere words but on the meaning behind them;
> Do not rely on the literal meaning but on the definitive meaning;
> Do not rely on the gross consciousness but on the exalted wisdom which realizes the meaning.

Thus, the Buddha himself has insisted that we analyze his own words.

One should decide which school is superior not by quoting from scriptures alone, but through logical reasoning.

Like the Mind-Only School, (*Chittamatra*, also known as *Yogachara*), the Middle Way School accepts the selflessness of phenomena, whereas the Followers of Scripture and the Great Exposition Schools do not.

The two latter schools, called schools of the Lesser Vehicle, assert that phenomena have self, or inherent existence.

Of the former two schools, the Mind-Only characterizes phenomena as being merely produced by an imprint on the mind.

The Middle Way School is divided into two branches. The Middle Way Autonomists (*Madhyamika Svatantrika*) say that all phenomena are imputed by terms and concepts but exist inherently. The Middle Way Consequentialists say that phenomena are selfless, exist conventionally but do not have inherent existence.

According to reasoning, ultimate truth is discovered by an analytical consciousness searching for the reality of phenomena, while conventional truth is discovered by a non-analytical consciousness searching for the same.

From the perspective of conventional truth, a book, for example, appears to have its own independent, inherent self-existence. It is an object which we can pick up, turn the pages and read the words of. We think conventionally that it has an essence which we call 'book'.

Yet searching further for this essence we realize that 'book' is merely the collection of its parts, that its whole is comprised of the parts of its form, such as colour and shape; and of its functions, like conveying the meaning of ideas or, when placed on top of a pile of papers, preventing them from blowing off our desk.

Each of the parts of the book can be further dissected into parts: the colour, for example, into ink and the paper on which it is applied, *ad infinitum.*

We can understand the book only as the whole of its parts. When we search for its essence we do not find it.

This is true of all phenomena. They do exist, but only on the level of conventional truth.

On the level of ultimate truth, phenomena exist only independence on other factors. All phenomena exist in the condition called dependent arising. When we try to discover their essence, we find only labels posited by conceptual thought, giving them their designations such as 'book'. Further, the consciousness which thus labels is dependent upon earlier and succeeding moments of consciousness, the beginning of which is nowhere to be found. There is no initial, inherently self-existent basis for such imputation.

Let us consider another example, something more abstract than 'book.' What do we mean when we designate an object 'long' or 'short'? When we look at our fingers, the ring finger is long in comparison to the little finger, but is short in comparison to the middle finger. The quality of length of the ring finger is posited independence on the other two fingers. The ring finger has no independent quality of length.

By contemplating along these lines, we realize that things exist in the nature of dependence, in the condition of dependent arising.

When we use this analysis on ourselves, two types of selflessness are explained: the selflessness of the person who experiences and perceives phenomena; and of the phenomena which are experienced and perceived. In other words, selflessness of the person and selflessness of phenomena.

The Self

There are many different systems by which we posit the conventional self. In some non-Buddhist writings the self is explained as a phenomenon which is permanent, pervasive, is never subject to change or destruction, and is a separate entity from the aggregates. From the Buddhist viewpoint such a self does not exist.

According to Buddhist scripture, the self exists from within the aggregates and not as something unrelated or coming from elsewhere.

The five aggregates are classified into two categories: body and mind.

We have an innate feeling that this body is our own possession. We posit this body as belonging to the self. In the same way, we have an innate feeling of 'my mind,' so that the mind too is looked upon as belonging to the self. Therefore we consider the self to be different from the body and the mind. Although we do this, when analytically sought, the self cannot be found apart from the body and the mind.

On the other hand, if this self did not exist at all, there would be no human beings.

Thus since the self does exist, yet we cannot find it when we search for it analytically, this indicates that it does not exist independently.

In the writings of the Middle Way, it is called a mere label or imputation that is not substantial.

We must recognize that although things appear to us as independently existent, that appearance contradicts the conclusion that we reach through investigation.

Why is the investigative conclusion more valid in our lives? Belief in appearance gives rise to grasping at its supposed independent existence, which in turn gives rise to emotions like desire and attachment. Refutation of the appearance of true existence by understanding its inconsistencies can prevent such negative emotions from arising.

All negative states of mind have their root in the self-grasping attitude, a mistaken consciousness which can be shown to be distorted. By refuting grasping at true existence, one can cut the roots of all delusions.

The prevention of delusions can be looked at as occurring in three stages.

One first has to refrain from their manifestations, which are misuse of the body and speech. Secondly, one must work toward abandoning the delusions themselves in the mind. Finally in the third stage, one works toward the elimination of imprints left by the delusions.

Through these three stages we achieve the following results. Refraining from misbehaviour of body and speech, we take rebirth in a higher state as human beings. Abandoning all delusions, we achieve nirvana or liberation. Thirdly abandoning even the imprints left behind by delusion, we achieve the omniscient state. Thus we follow the path.

The path is explained briefly in the three higher trainings.

First comes the training in self-discipline, the practice of restraining the body and speech from negative ways. By this restraint, one prevents gross distractions.

The second training, that of single-pointed concentration, or calm abiding meditation, achieves a state of mind free from the subtlest distractions.

When such single-pointed concentration is used in the third training, meditation on the nature of emptiness, it becomes special insight, or transcendent wisdom.

These three higher trainings free us from the three types of suffering.

Having passed beyond the state of the desire realm and having achieved the form realm via training in self-discipline, one becomes free from the suffering of suffering. Secondly through the practice of calm abiding meditation one transcends the form realms and achieves liberation from the suffering of change, which is the experience of pleasure becoming pain. Instead one always remains in a transcendent state.

Thirdly, through understanding the real nature of all realms of existence, one achieves freedom from the suffering of conditioned existence.

Questions and Answers

Question: Consequentialists state that phenomena exist merely by implication. If that is true, does it not refute the external existence of the object?

His Holiness: When Middle Way Consequentialists speak about phenomena as existing as mere imputations, this does not refute external objects, the phenomena which are not names. Rather, it suggests that phenomena generally are not perceived by valid cognition.

When Middle Way Consequentialists come to the conclusion that the essence of a phenomenon cannot be found when searched for analytically, this is not an indication of its non-existence but rather of its non-inherent existence.

As explained in the opening verse of *The Fundamental Treatise on Wisdom* by Nagarjuna, the examination of a phenomenon, which on the conventional level has such qualities as going and coming, or production and cessation, refutes inherent existence.

One can say that this table is non-inherently existent because it is existent, since it exists depending on other factors. The very fact of its existence proves its non-inherent existence.

On the other hand, when Yogacarins of the Mind-Only School search analytically for the existence of external objects by dissecting or analysing the parts of an object, and do not find the whole, they say that external objects do not exist as separate entities from the consciousness. Their answer is that an object is of the same substance as consciousness. Therefore they say there are no external objects. Then they assert that internal consciousness is truly existent, is independent.

Question: Can you give us a short explanation of the debate between the Indian pandit Kamalashila and the Chinese master Hashang?

His Holiness: During the time of Pandit Shantarakshita there were Chinese masters called Hashangs in Tibet. At Samye there were different buildings for translators, tantric practitioners, and meditators. The Hashangs stayed in the building called 'Abode of Immovable Concentration,' a special place for meditators.

At that time the Hashangs' main practice was meditation. There was nothing wrong with the ways of the Hashangs; they simply were experts in meditation. But there is a statement in a sutra to the effect that through conceptual thought or preconception one cannot achieve release or liberation; and during the time of Kamalashila some Hashangs misinterpreted this passage, thinking that any type of conceptual thought is a fault of the mind.

It is true that when, in highest yoga tantra, one engages in the practice or the experience of the subjective clear light, one has to prevent the arising of all conceptual thought because it would harm or affect the practitioner in his or her effort to bring all the subtle energies into the main channel.

But the reason for preventing all conceptual thought at this stage is not that all conceptual thought is mistaken or is a distorted consciousness grasping at true existence.

Rather, at that stage, as one makes an all-out effort to bring all the energies into the main channel, even positive thoughts will affect the absorptive state, as long as they are conceptual and analytical.

Not understanding this, some of the Hashang scholars took it to mean that all conceptual thoughts are distorted and have the nature of grasping at true existence. Therefore, the confusion arose.

We might have some very special reasons for the prevention of conceptual thought, but if we prevented all types of conceptual thought apart from distorted misconceptions, there would be no way of cultivating wisdom.

This is how I interpret the debate. If we were to say that the Hashangs were entirely wrong, then why should Shantirakshita have given permission for the debate? And if we say that all the views of the Hashangs were correct, then why should Kamalashila have refuted them?

Question: I have a question regarding the relationship between *vipashyana* and tantric meditation.

I find that *vipashyana*, which establishes an understanding of impermanence in our mind, is a step towards selflessness. But tantric meditation on external forms I find to be distracting. How does it fit in with the simplicity of arriving at selflessness?

His Holiness: I will explain this later. But let me say now that tantric practice is difficult, not at all easy.

It has a special significance, special purpose, for in the Tantrayana the mind practises two virtues simultaneously.

When, in Sutrayana, the mind concentrates on emptiness, at that moment we accumulate one kind of virtue. In that state we accumulate stores of wisdom; but during that state we cannot accumulate stores of merit. At other times, when we practise development of the mind of enlightenment or compassion, we accumulate the other type of merit; but during that moment wisdom cannot develop.

In tantric practice, the wisdom which understands emptiness itself transforms into deities. The mandalas, appearances as a deity, penetrate into the ultimate nature of being, emptiness. That wisdom creates both virtues simultaneously.

That is the special significance of tantric practice. It is quite easy to explain, but very difficult to accomplish.

This tantric practice can also be categorized as *vipashyana* practice. There are many levels of *vipashyana* practice.

Question: Please give your opinion on the understanding of impermanence and momentariness. Many of our institutions in society, such as marriage, government and so forth, are based on an acceptance of a certain regularity in the structure of relationships. If you have the right view according to Middle Way philosophy, then these institutions seem to become redundant, unnecessary, and even to come into conflict with practice.

His Holiness: On the subject of impermanence, as long as there is a phenomenon which is the product of a cause it is susceptible to changes produced by the cause itself.

Look at this table. We saw it yesterday, but in substance it is no longer the same today. And this book; it is here now but yesterday's book has already disappeared.

All phenomena undergo a steady change: day by day, moment by moment, second by second. This is also confirmed by the analysis of subatomic particles; there is a continual change.

That kind of changing nature is always there, without any special order or cause to stop the previous nature. The very cause which produced this book also produced its changed nature. For example, eye-consciousness is active as long as the eye-organ is there, but as soon as this eye-organ is damaged or dies, then that consciousness is no more.

The same is true of a human being's consciousness, or a Tibetan consciousness.

These consciousnesses exist only momentarily. But my main consciousness, the sixth mental consciousness, the deeper level of consciousness, is always there. It is beginningless and endless, and although it changes momentarily, from the viewpoint of continuity it is a permanent entity.

In human society momentary change is quite obvious. Food is changing, behaviour is changing, fashion is changing, education is changing. Yet as a whole the continuity of human society is always there.

All these phenomena which are products of causes are impermanent from the viewpoint of momentary change, but they are eternal from the viewpoint of their continuity.

As for your question about remaining detached to things because they are impermanent, if we have to detach ourselves from things simply because they are impermanent, then we should give up the spiritual path we are seeking, because it too is impermanent.

The issue is not whether a phenomena is impermanent or permanent; it is whether or not it is worthwhile to feel a desire for or to achieve something; and if so, how to fulfil that desire.

We must make a distinction between proper and improper desire. When we find through investigative reasoning that a desire is worth fulfilling, then having that kind of desire can be useful. For example, the desire to achieve Buddhahood and the desire to work for the benefit of all sentient beings are both beneficial desires.

These desires we should deliberately try to develop in our minds. We should make a special effort to develop the feeling that all sentient beings are 'mine.'

On the other hand, you often desire something, but when you think about it more deeply you find that you do not really need it. For example, when you go to a supermarket you see plenty of good things there; and you want all of them. Then you count your money, and the second thought comes to your mind: do you really need all that? Your answer? Not necessary.

That is my own experience. Such improper desire is really attachment, greed, for things not really necessary to live comfortably, to survive.

To wish with sufficient reason and to acquire one or two things, that is proper desire.

For a layman, family life is normal. But considering it in relation to cultivating a path to achieve liberation, one must be careful not to fall under the sway of delusions.

Caution is also necessary if a good practitioner remains a monk or nun.

Under certain circumstances, people may judge that this exceptional person has less influence and is less useful in society than he or she would be as a lay person. In that role, he or she could be a good practitioner but also a good member of society, a productive person earning a livelihood, a good, honorable person, with inner peace that would create a peaceful atmosphere within his or her own family and the community.

Such a person with the mind of enlightenment, an altruistic, attitude, under certain circumstances can in fact be more useful to society as a lay person in family life.

However, if one wants to achieve the path chiefly for one's own concern or benefit, then the way of a monk or nun is recommended for its simplicity of lifestyle. And for the practice of the mind of enlightenment, taking into account the welfare of all other sentient beings, both leading a family life and being a monk or nun can be recommended.

Question: What is the difference between renunciation and running away from life?

His Holiness: There are big differences. But for a practitioner who is working towards the achievement of liberation chiefly for himself, these two could sometimes be more or less the same.

Running away from worldly life because one is disturbed is not good. There are, for example, some people who, due to depression or some unpleasantness, commit suicide; this is really tragic.

The third category of suffering, its ultimate source, is our body. The actual way to escape suffering is cessation of samsaric rebirth. Rebirth happens not due to God or some other force but through one's own ignorance, a state of mind which grasps at things in a distorted way.

Bodhisattva practitioners should deliberately and actively live in situations where there is trouble, because they are chiefly working for the welfare of other sentient beings.

However, there is the element of timing. At the initial stage, a practitioner might develop very strong altruism, but he may still be very young for such a determination. At a tender age there exists the danger of influence by unfavorable external conditions that can undermine one's determination.

At that time complete isolation for a certain period may be necessary for the development of inner strength.

Once one has developed that inner strength, then one should deliberately go out into society, and remain in troubled places and help.

Question: Is it socially dangerous to teach people to renounce the world, to go away from it?

His Holiness: Simply running away is dangerous. On the other hand, if a few people give up society induced by a sincere motivation to seek the truth or path, they do not make much difference. But a large number of people leaving society might have a negative effect on the community.

Questioner: I think it might be dangerous to teach someone who is young because he might not understand the context of what you are saying. For him, renunciation might merely mean not to stay with his wife, not to drink beer. It might be better for him to stay in the city than to go into the mountains where he thinks he is virtuous and his ego gets dangerously bigger and bigger.

His Holiness: It is very wrong to take hasty actions. We must first investigate thoroughly. Do not be like the practitioner who suddenly renounces even eating because of the force of his effort, but after three days suddenly abandons all spiritual practice.

Yet to give up society, and with a sincere motivation and in the correct way remain in a solitary meditation place, can be of great benefit. Without the practice of meditative absorption and single-pointedness of the mind, our ordinary sixth mental consciousness cannot develop sharp wisdom.

So we must experience that kind of meditation, for which solitude is necessary. One must go to a remote place and practise for a long period, for a few years. Once one has developed single-pointedness of mind, one comes back.

At present some Tibetans remain in the mountains practising with great effort. But without any self-understanding, some people merely pretend that they are doing a religious practice, and are in fact neither a monk nor a family person.

There is a Tibetan saying that when a bat is among birds he pretends to be a mouse, and when he is among mice he pretends to be a bird.

Question: What kind of a middle path would Your Holiness recommend so that ordinary aspirants can see the way without the complexity of higher aspirations?

His Holiness: In order to achieve liberation, first of all one must develop the strong wish to do so. It is necessary to identify and reflect on suffering.

The chief suffering to which we are referring is the suffering of conditioned existence.

Not everything that is impermanent is in the nature of suffering. For example, the omniscient mind of the Buddha, although impermanent, is not in the nature of suffering.

But our mental and physical aggregates are impermanent. That is, they are subject to change, and are the product of causes. Cause in this case refers to contaminated actions we have committed, our karma, and also the delusions which induced them. Because form is the product of this impermanence, it is in the nature of suffering.

Our lives begin with the suffering of birth. During conception and after entering the womb, the process of physical development begins. The form becomes grosser and grosser. At a certain stage one starts to experience pleasure and pain, and at the time of actual birth, the real suffering begins. From that point for a considerable time we remain as helpless as insects. This is how our lives begin.

Although the birth of a child is celebrated, this is the beginning of his real suffering. This lifetime ends with death, also an undesired suffering. Between these two events, we experience the sufferings of illness and aging.

We need a purpose in this life to give it meaning beyond feeding this suffering body. We should ask ourselves if the sustenance of our body is the whole purpose or essence of this life. If we can bring about a transformation of the mind which inhabits this body, then there is a kind of purpose.

Rationally speaking, our body is not at all an object worthy to be cherished or attached to. No matter how beautiful or how strong, the body's real substances, like skin, bones and flesh, when analyzed, are not beautiful. They are impure. Its substances are unclean. The body itself is unclean, and it is also the product of unclean substances. The cause of this body is the two regenerative fluids of the parents, which are also unclean. The body produces faeces and urine. In a way it is a machine to produce faeces and urine. That is its main purpose, to consume food and drink, then produce waste.

If I think of the amount of food and drink, like Tibetan tea and tsampa, that I have consumed in fifty-two years, it seems that the main purpose of my body has been to produce human waste. At the same time, if we were to put all the discharges like mucus together they would come to quite a lot. Nobody regards a toilet as something clean, do they? Actually, an individual is a toilet. The things in the toilet do not come from the sky. They come from the body.

Fortunately, however, with this body we have the human mind. If we can utilize the power of the intelligence with which human beings are endowed, then we can make our lives purposeful. That we are able to think, to analyze, gives us a great opportunity.

We can note that a limited kind of altruism can be developed by animals and insects. Bees and ants, for example, are by nature social insects. In good or bad times, their entire social structure works toward survival. They have to depend on one another, and they display what we would call responsibility and genuine cooperation.

Human nature is also like that. In order to survive we have to depend on others whether we like it or not.

If we think about this, we will find that naturally we need love. We are born and grow up through the kindness of parents. We are still alive because of our parents' kindness and human warmth. As we get older and become weaker mentally and physically, we again depend on the kindness of others. Between these two stages, while we are strong and healthy, we tend to forget these facts. This is a kind of ignorance.

The most basic human requirement is human warmth, a warm heart.

It is quite clear that we need friends. Through friends we get mental happiness and mental peace. In order to form real friendships, we have to utilize positive human thoughts, such as love, compassion, and a warm heart. With these we can create genuine friendship.

Many of our ordinary friends are not always genuine. When we have power and money, then we have many friends; but when this power and money disappear, those friends also disappear.

The true friends that we find through a good heart will remain friends whether we have success or face failure and problems. That kind of friendship can develop only through a genuine good heart.

The basic fact is that humanity survives through kindness, love and compassion. That human beings can develop these qualities is their real blessing.

We have gained this human form. Were we to use the intelligence human beings are endowed with by utilizing the potential of this warm heart that we have, then we would find the real fulfillment, the purpose of human life.

Thinking about it from our own point of view, we will find that, as long as we possess these mental and physical aggregates, which are the product of our own contaminated actions and delusions, there is no possibility for everlasting peace and happiness. And we will find that all other sentient beings are in the same situation.

So we must generate a genuine aspiration to achieve enlightenment, a state which is free from the bonds of delusions and karma. That can be called renunciation, although one does not renounce society or family. While we work for the benefit of other sentient beings, the fulfillment of our own welfare comes as a by-product.

In order to train oneself in the development of an altruistic mind, the Indian masters evolved two major systems. One is the seven-point cause and effect method, and the other is called the exchange and equalizing of oneself with others.

A preliminary to the first of the seven points is the cultivation of equanimity, that is to say, a state of mind which tries to equalize strong attachment for friends, strong hatred for enemies, and indifference towards neutral people.

The actual first step is that, remembering our own beginningless rebirths, we recognize that all sentient beings have at one time or another been our mothers, friends and relatives.

Then secondly, having recognized them as such, we recollect and reflect on the kindness they have extended to us.

Step three is to repay their kindness.

We develop the determination to repay kindnesses by reflecting how our mother of this lifetime extends her kindness to us and how other parents extend their kindness to their children.

Loving-kindness is step four. This state of mind cherishes all sentient beings.

In the fifth step, having developed this loving kindness for all sentient beings, we wish for all sentient beings to be free from suffering. That is compassion.

Sixthly comes the unusual attitude of universal responsibility, the attitude to take on ourselves the responsibility to free sentient beings from suffering.

The seventh step in this method of cultivating the altruistic attitude to achieve Buddhahood is that of generating the thought of enlightenment.

This thought of enlightenment is experienced partly by the force of our strong compassion for all sentient beings and partly by the understanding that it is possible for the minds of sentient beings to be freed from their delusions. All sentient beings have the potential to achieve the state of omniscience. Understanding this, and a strong force of compassion, bring about the experience of the thought of enlightenment.

The second system, exchanging and equalizing oneself with others, begins again with the cultivation of equanimity, but in a different way.

According to this method, one takes the point of view of sentient beings. One considers how all sentient beings are equal in the sense that they all wish to achieve happiness and avoid suffering. We all have this same wish. Thus one equalizes oneself with others.

Next one reflects on the disadvantages of cherishing oneself.

When a person is selfish and wants all happiness for himself, in the end he acquires many enemies and few friends. On the other hand, if we exchange ourselves for others, if we cherish others and hold them dearer than ourselves, we will experience the opposite results. We will have more friends and fewer enemies.

In short, just as Shantideva said in his *A Guide to the Bodhisattva Ways* "All the frustrations we find in this world are the product of cherishing ourselves, and all happiness the product of cherishing others." Thus, one reflects on the disadvantages of self-cherishing and the advantages of cherishing others.

Next follows the practice of giving and taking, by which method we again cultivate the mind of enlightenment. We meditate on giving away goodness and happiness, and taking on the hardships of others.

These days, when we (Tibetans) undertake the practice of cultivating the mind of enlightenment, we combine the two above systems.

One overall effect of these methods is that even enemies come to be regarded as being very kind.

Quite simply, in order to develop genuine altruism you need to control anger and hatred. This control requires the practice of patience and tolerance. In order to develop patience and tolerance, you need an enemy. To think thus is to make use of the enemy, irrespective of his or her motivations.

When one is capable of seeing the enemy as helpful and kind, then there is no question of whether or not one can see others in the same light.

All objects of worldly desire, like fame, wealth, and health, depend on the kindness of others and are fulfilled by them. Even the possibility of our coming together here and having this discussion was brought about through the contribution of many others: those who built this house, wove the carpets and so forth. The bus in which you came, despite some troubles in the Punjab, is another factor which brought us together here.

Without these factors we would not have had the opportunity to meet. Without people we know and don't know, we could not have met.

Think on these lines, and you will develop the conviction that without the help of others you cannot survive.

Think also about karma. Our present opportunity is the product of our own past positive karma. And also think about what is meant by positive karma. Generally this is something we create motivated by the wish to benefit others, so even the accumulation of that karma requires others as the basis.

Of all Buddhist practices, cultivating the mind of enlightenment is regarded as the most precious.

Meditation on the mind of enlightenment has its root in compassion, and without sentient beings we cannot develop compassion. We might get blessings from the Buddhas for the development of the mind of enlightenment, but we cannot cultivate compassion by focusing on them. It is only possible to develop compassion by focusing on sentient beings.

From this point of view, sentient beings are kinder than the Buddhas. It is not necessary for the other sentient beings to have a good motivation. For example, many objects which we regard as valuable, like cessation and the path, do not have a good motivation, yet we cherish and value them.

For the practitioner of the Bodhisattva path, all sentient beings are his friends and all environments are conducive to practice. The only actual enemy is the self-grasping attitude and consequent distorted mind.

When one practises in such a way, one gains freedom from fear.

3

Two Essential Texts

Manjushri, Bodhisattva of Wisdom

At this point I would like to use two simple texts as the basis of our discussion.

The first of these is known as *The Eight Verses for Training the mind*, and deals with the principles of developing the Bodhisattva spirit. It was written many centuries ago.

The second text is *A Tantric Meditation Simplified for Beginners*, a short meditational text I myself wrote some years ago. (*Note: The editors have included this text as an appendix to the present volume.*)

♦

Eight Verses for Training the Mind

I received an oral transmission and teachings on *The Eight Verses for Training the Mind* from Kyabje Trijang Rinpoche, my late Junior Tutor. I have been reciting these verses every day for more than thirty-five years, and contemplating their meanings.

The composer of this text, the Kadampa master Geshe Langri Thangpa, saw the practice of the mind of enlightenment, and in particular the meditation of exchanging self with others, as most important throughout his life.

I shall explain the eight verses briefly:

> With the determination to accomplish
> The highest welfare of all sentient beings,
> Who excel even the wish-fulfilling jewel,
> May I at all times hold them dear.

Sentient beings' kindness to us is not confined to the achievement of our final goal, enlightenment. The fulfillment of our temporary aims, such as the experience of happiness, also depends on their kindness.

Therefore sentient beings are superior even to the wish-fulfilling jewel. So we make the prayer, 'May I at all times hold them dear.' We should regard them as being more precious than a wish-fulfilling jewel.

> Whenever I associate with others
> May I think of myself as the lowest of all
> And from the depth of my heart
> Hold the others as supreme.

When we meet others we should not think of ourselves as superior and look down on or pity them, but think of ourselves as more humble than they are. We should hold them dear and revere them because they have a capacity equal to the activities of the Buddhas to grant us happiness and enlightenment.

> In all actions may I search into my mind,
> And as soon as delusions arise
> That endanger myself and others,
> May I firmly face and avert them.

When we engage in ritual practice, we sometimes encounter obstacles. These obstacles are not external but internal; they are delusions of our own mind. The real enemy, the destroyer of our happiness, is within ourselves.

When through training and effort we are able to discipline and control our mind, then we will gain real peace and tranquillity.

Therefore Buddha said, "You are your own master." Everything rests on your own shoulders, depends on yourself.

Although in the practice of the mind of enlightenment we have to restrain from all negative ways, primarily we must avoid anger. Anger can never produce happiness, whereas attachment can bring about the experience of happiness in certain cases.

We have a saying in Tibet: "If you lose your temper and get angry, bite your knuckles." This means that if you lose your temper, do not show it to others; rather say to yourself, "Leave it."

> When I see beings of wicked nature,
> Oppressed by violent misdeeds and afflictions,
> May I hold them dear
> As if I had found a rare and precious treasure.

Some people, when they see others who are exhausted by sufferings and oppressed by delusions, tend to avoid these experiences because they are afraid of getting involved and carried away. Bodhisattvas, instead of avoiding such situations, face them bravely as an opportunity to bring happiness to other sentient beings.

> When others out of envy treat me badly
> With slander, abuse and the like,
> May I suffer the loss and
> Offer the victory to them.

When other beings, especially those who hold a grudge against you, abuse and harm you out of envy, you should not abandon them, but hold them as objects of your greatest compassion and take care of them.

Thus the practitioner should take the 'loss' on himself or herself, and offer the 'victory' to the others.

Practitioners of the mind of enlightenment take the loss on themselves and offer the victory to others, not with the motivation to become virtuous themselves but rather with the motivation to help other sentient beings.

Since it is sometimes possibly, however, that taking the loss and offering the victory to others can harm them in the long run, there are cases when you should not do it.

If a practitioner of altruism finds himself in such a situation, then induced by a strong motive to help others, he should actually do the opposite.

Think in these terms. When something unpleasant happens and you get irritated, you are the loser, since irritation immediately destroys your own mental peace and in the long run brings unwanted results. Yet if someone hurts you and you do not lose your mental peace, that is a victory.

If you become impatient and lose your temper, then you lose the best part of the human brain, judgement of the situation. Once you are angry, almost mad with anger, then you cannot make correct decisions.

When your mind is calm you can analyze in a clearer way. Without losing your tranquillity, analyze the circumstances, and if necessary take counteractions. This is the spiritual meaning of loss and victory.

> When the one whom I have helped
> And benefited with great hope
> Hurts me badly, may I behold him
> As my supreme guru.

When one among those whom you have benefited repays your kindness in the wrong way, you might feel that you do not want to help him ever again. For the very reason that it is difficult not to hold this against him—and this is a great stumbling block for the practitioner of altruism—it is emphasized that a practitioner should care specially for such a person.

A person who harms you should be seen not only as someone who needs your special care, but also as someone who is your spiritual guide. You will find that your enemy is your supreme teacher.

> In short, may I directly and indirectly offer
> Benefit and happiness to all my mothers.
> May I secretly take upon myself the harmful actions
> And suffering of my mothers.

Since others are infinite in number, and since you yourself are only one, no matter how superior you are, others become the more valuable. If you have some power of judgment, you will find that it is worthwhile to sacrifice yourself for the sake of others, that one person must not sacrifice infinite numbers of others for the sake of oneself.

Special visualization is valuable here. See yourself as a very selfish person, and in front of you a great number of sentient beings undergoing their sufferings. Visualize them actively experiencing their sufferings while you selfishly remain neutral and unbiased. Then see which side you want to take, theirs or your own.

If selfish politicians thought like this, then they would without hesitation join the majority.

Initially it is very difficult to decrease and control your selfish attitude. But if you persevere for a long time, you will be successful.

He who from the depth of his heart practices taking onto himself all the suffering and faults of the other sentient beings should also train in sharing with them all good qualities like virtues and happiness that he has in himself.

The above seven verses deal with the practice of the conventional mind of enlightenment, which is method. The eighth verse deals with the practice of the ultimate mind of enlightenment, which is wisdom.

By engaging in the practice of the conventional mind of enlightenment, one accumulates a store of merit; and by engaging in the practice of the ultimate mind of enlightenment one accumulates a store of wisdom.

With these two forces combined, one achieves as a result the two bodies of the Buddha: the Form Body, or *Rupakaya*; and the Truth Body, or *Dharmakaya*.

> May all this remain undefiled by the stains of
> Keeping in view the eight worldly principles.
> May I, by perceiving all phenomena as illusory,
> Unattached, be delivered from the bondage of samsara.

If someone undertakes such a practice motivated by worldly concerns like wishing for a long and healthy life in which he has happiness and achieves perfection, this is basically wrong. To undertake the practice hoping that people will call one a great religious practitioner is also definitely wrong. So is viewing the objects of one's compassion as truly existent.

You should undertake this practice with the understanding that all phenomena are like illusions.

One understands that all phenomena are like illusions through negating their supposedly true existence, leaving behind what is mere imputation, label, designation. This is the Buddhist view.

Earlier we talked about view and conduct in Buddhism. This view is called dependent arising. Although there are many different levels of meaning to dependent arising, its final meaning approaches the understanding of emptiness.

Dependent arising establishes the evidence of something as not truly existent. By gaining a complete understanding of dependent arising, one has the strong conviction of the functioning of the conventions. Therefore one engages in the practice of the mind of enlightenment and accumulates the store of merit; and by focusing on emptiness, or non-true existence, one accumulates the store of wisdom.

Supported by this strong motivation of the mind of enlightenment, one engages in the practice of the six perfections, or *paramitas*: generosity, discipline, patience, joyous effort, concentration and wisdom.

The six perfections can also be considered under three headings as the three higher trainings.

The first of the three higher trainings is the practice of discipline. There are three ways to effect this. The one explained in the *Pratimoksha* or *Vinaya* is called individual liberation. The second is the discipline of Bodhisattvas, and the third the discipline of tantra.

The discipline of individual liberation is of two types, that of monks and that of lay-people.

Lay-people can take two types of precepts, either for one day or for the rest of their life.

All of the vows are based on refraining from the ten negative courses of action: killing, stealing, and sexual misconduct (these three being non-virtues of the body); lying, derisive talk, harsh words, and idle gossip (these four being verbal non-virtuous actions); and covetousness, harmful intent, and wrong views (the three non-virtuous actions of the mind).

The wrong views referred to are chiefly nihilistic views, but there are also other wrong view, like acceptance of an almighty creator.

The chief way to practice the discipline of the Bodhisattvas is to refrain from cherishing oneself more than others. There are many different Bodhisattva precepts.

Within the discipline of tantra, there are four classes of tantra; and for the two highest tantras, certain precepts have to be taken and observed. The main precepts are to refrain from ordinary appearances and from grasping at ordinariness.

In the practice of these three disciplines, the lower one should be taken as the basis for the next higher one. Having laid the foundation for discipline, one has to engage in the practice of the two remaining higher trainings: meditation and wisdom.

Although techniques for the practice of meditation and wisdom are explained in the Mahayana sutras, the techniques explained in tantra are considered by Tibetan Buddhists to be superior.

A Tantric Meditation

Some years ago I compiled a booklet entitled *A Tantric Meditation Simplified for Beginners* (see *Appendix*) for new Buddhists who had not received any tantric initiations but who had an interest in the practice.

It is not necessary to explain the opening verses. We will start from the paragraph headed 'Visualization' where the following directions are given, "In the space before your forehead visualize...." and so forth, for the visualization of the five deities: Lord Buddha in the centre, surrounded by Avalokiteshvara, Vajrapani, Manjushri and Arya Tara.

Note here that although Buddhists refute the theory of an almighty creator, in Buddhism, and especially in tantric Buddhism, there are numerous mandalas and deities. One interpretation of these is that an enlightened being can appear in different aspects, as exemplified by the Buddha himself. He assumed the Form Body for the benefit of others, to whom it is visible. The aspect, colour and shape in which this Form Body appears depends on the mental faculties or dispositions of the sentient beings.

Although in nature the Form Body is the omniscient wisdom of the Buddha, due to the varying circumstances and mental faculties of sentient beings, it appears in different aspects. On the other hand, the

Truth Body is not a form which is visible or accessible to others but rather is a state actualized by the enlightened beings.

In the *Kalachakra Tantra*, the more than seven hundred deities are in reality manifestations of a Buddha's mental qualities.

Here Avalokiteshvara is the manifestation of the Buddhas' compassion; Manjushri is the manifestation of their wisdom; Vajrapani is the manifestation of their energy or karma; and Tara, as a female deity, is the manifestation of their power to motivate action.

According to highest yoga tantra, Buddha's two main disciples, Shariputra and Maudgalyayana, are also deities or Bodhisattvas. But generally speaking they are regarded as beings separate from Buddha.

To resume visualizing: Buddha sits on a lotus throne in the centre, in the vajra posture, right hand in the earth-touching mudra, left hand holding a begging bowl at the level of the navel. On either side of the throne and a little to the front stand Shariputra and Maudgalyayana.

The Dharma is the complete abandonment of both delusions and obscurations of the paths. Thus it is associated with consciousness itself, and therefore is formless. But you visualize it in the form of scriptures, on a table to the right of the Buddha. Then visualize the formless omniscient mind of the Buddha as a stupa, to the Buddha's left.

The scriptures to the right of the Buddha (the nature of cessations and paths within the Buddha) and the stupa to the left of the Buddha (the representation of the omniscient mind) are the Dharma.

Thus one recollects the three objects of refuge, the Three Jewels: Buddha in the centre and the Bodhisattvas around him as the spiritual community, the Sangha.

Of these three, the actual refuge is the Dharma, because when we realize the Dharma in our mind, we achieve freedom from sufferings. Therefore Dharma is the actual refuge which protects us.

In order to experience the realization of the Dharma in our own mind, we need someone to guide us. This is the teacher, the Buddha.

In order to actualize such a Dharma, we require spiritual companions, examples to emulate; this is the spiritual community, the Sangha.

Since the practice of taking refuge is undertaken in conjunction with the practice of altruism, we need love and compassion for all sentient beings.

For this reason visualize around you all sentient beings. Your enemies are in front of you because they are dearest to you, not because they might run away if you visualized them behind you.

At this point of your visualization, reflect deeply and thoroughly on the cultivation of altruism, how sentient beings lack happiness and how they suffer acutely.

When we talk of sentient beings we should not think of them as far away but begin by thinking of those around us, like family and neighbours. Otherwise when we talk of the objects of compassion, we think of them as objects to be quarreled with.

Now think that, in order to free ourselves from suffering and its cause, we must convince ourselves that it is necessary for all sentient beings to realize the nature of reality, the actual refuge within ourselves.

With such a motivation recite the refuge mantra: *'Namo Buddhaya, Namo Dharmaya, Namo Sanghaya.'* Do this three, twenty-one, or a hundred times.

The sound of the recitation is not as important as the strong motivation and determination. When you have developed them, recite the above words of refuge.

After having taken refuge, one should offer the seven-limbed prayer as explained in the booklet (see *Appendix*)

Now concentrate for a while on the Buddha and the sacred objects.

When you have a clear picture of them in your mind, visualize a flat, luminous circle in the centre of the chest of each deity.

In each circle is the symbolic syllable of the respective deity: *Mum* for Buddha, *Hrih* for Avalokiteshvara, *Dhih* for Manjushri, *Hum* for Vajrapani, and *Tam* for Tara. Each seed syllable is surrounded by its mantra.

At this point I shall give an oral transmission of the mantras. Please repeat after me three times:-

Om muni muni maha muniye svaha–the mantra of Buddha;
Om mani padme hum–the mantra of Avalokiteshvara;
Om wagi shvari mum–the mantra of Manjushri;
Om vajra pani hum–the mantra of Vajrapani;
Om tara tuttare ture svaha–the mantra of Tara.

Recite these mantras as often as you can. During the recitation reflect on the cultivation of altruism, on love, on the kindness of sentient beings, and on compassion.

In this way you can develop a strong feeling for the three objects of refuge. Visualize light-rays radiating from the deities.

The mantra of Lord Buddha is the main one: *Om muni muni mahamune ye svaha*. It signifies the control of enlightenment.

Since Avalokiteshvara is the physical manifestation of the great compassion of the Buddhas, practitioners who emphasize cultivation of compassion should concentrate on the recitation of *Om mani padme hum*. This mantra is also recited in memory of people who have passed away.

Manjushri is the physical manifestation of the Buddhas' wisdom and intelligence. Therefore the recitation of his mantra, *Om wagi shvari mum*, is very helpful to students and especially children during the time of their education. If someone is involved in a court case where he needs sharp and clever answers, this mantra might also help.

Vajrapani is the physical manifestation of all the energies and actions of the Buddhas, and the recitation of his mantra, *Om vajra pani hum*, is helpful in dispersing obstacles. Although practitioners of the Dharma should not be superstitious, this mantra is said to be helpful for preventing harms caused by other-dimensional beings.

Tara is said to be the purified aspect of our energy-winds. The energy factor moves the consciousness onto its object and induces activities. Energy is a special, subtle force. When we seek the attainment of peace, health, and the increase of wealth or life-span, the recitation of *Om tara tuttare ture svaha* is very helpful.

If you are interested in the development of single-pointedness of the mind, you can cultivate it at this point in the meditation session.

The object of observation for this practice varies. One can focus on external objects, internal objects, on one's own mind, or on emptiness.

In training for meditative absorption we have to identify the five faults that prevent single-pointedness and apply the eight mental antidotes. Other techniques are explained in the nine mental stages of development, and the six powers and four attentions that bring progress. These can be studied from other books.

In short, the most important factors required for the cultivation of meditation are a steadfast and stable concentration, and absolute clarity of the object. The subjective mind should be very clear and alert.

Two of the faults which hinder the attainment of single-pointedness are gross mental excitement and gross mental sinking. To bring down excitement, it helps to reflect on suffering. If in the process of it our mind becomes too withdrawn or even depressed, then we have to uplift it by thinking of something stimulating or by going out into the open air, into the light to enjoy a pleasant view. In these ways one overcomes gross mental sinking and gross mental excitement.

Sometimes during meditation we find subtle manifestations of mental excitement or of sinking. We lose clarity of the object or intensity of concentration. It is not necessary to end the session. Just try to balance the mind.

When the mind is easily distracted it helps to meditate in a darkish room and to face a wall.

A person who seriously starts the practice of meditative absorption should have many sessions a day, up to twenty, each lasting about ten minutes, as if one were keeping the continuity of the fire without losing the heat.

If in long meditation sessions we experience subtle mental sinking and lose clarity of the object, we waste time. It is better to have short sessions at the initial stage.

One can see many meditators in impressive postures who are resting in mental dullness or mental sinking. As a consequence of too much mental sinking, the mind becomes duller and duller.

If you cultivate meditative absorption in the proper way and reach a stage where you can hold your object of meditation for a period of up to four hours without the fault of excitement or sinking, that is real progress. When you keep on with this meditation in a correct way, the breathing process may cease for certain periods.

Then meditate on emptiness, reflecting on the ultimate nature of the Buddha. Since all phenomena lack inherent existence, so the Buddhas in whom we take refuge also lack inherent existence. Just as we analyze ourselves, searching for the self, whether it is the body, the mind, etc., in the same way we analyze the Buddha.

If we try to find out whether the body of the Buddha is Buddha, whether the mind of the Buddha is Buddha, we do not find the Buddha. Although he exists, when we search for the essence of this designation, we cannot find Buddha together with or separate from the body or the mind. We have to come to the conclusion that Buddha is a mere label imputed on the composite of the mind and body of the person.

Then reflect how Buddha appears to your natural mind. You will find that, just as your self appears to you as solidly existing from its own side, so it appears to us as if Buddha existed in his own right. Reflect that if such a Buddha existed as he appears to you, you would be able to find his essence when you searched for it. But you cannot find it. So you have to come to the conclusion that Buddha does not exist as he appears to you.

To symbolize that all outer phenomena are in the nature of emptiness, visualize as follows. Avalokiteshvara dissolves into the Buddha's head, Manjushri into his throat, Vajrapani into his chest, Tara into his navel and the two chief disciples into the two sides of his body.

Retaining a clear visualization only of the Buddha, concentrate as long as you can. Then the Buddha melts slowly into light from top and bottom towards the heart, and is absorbed into a luminous circle at the centre of his heart.

The circle disappears into the mantra, the mantra into the symbolic letter *Mum* which it surrounds. Then the *Mum* also changes into light, and only the top of the Tibetan letter *Mum*, the *tigle* is left. Then that too vanishes slowly into emptiness.

Rest your mind for a moment on the emptiness of all self-existing appearance.

When you dissolve the Buddha's appearance into emptiness, you should not think that he does not exist at all. Rather, you should understand that he is empty of inherent existence.

Now you visualize that from a state of emptiness the Buddha and the other figures reappear. You keep them before you. Then close the meditation, and dedicate the merits.

Questions and Answers

Question: When you have reached the states of meditation as higher beings have, do you still have to go through the visualization of the Buddha and the holy throng like Tara and everybody else with all their attributes? Can't a person who has reached a higher state go to the Buddha directly through meditation?

His Holiness: In this kind of tantric practice, there are different kinds of meditation in which one can engage in relation to the different aspects of a Buddha's attributes. Therefore I gave an explanation of these different visualizations.

For the path it is actually not necessary to visualize the Buddha. Without any visualization, one can simply meditate on emptiness or on the mind of enlightenment.

Simply meditate on emptiness on the wisdom side, and the altruistic mind of enlightenment on the method side.

But for tantric practice, it is generally necessary to practise visualizations because the resultant state has the Form Body as well as the Truth Body.

The main reason we want to achieve Buddhahood is to help other sentient beings. The actual Buddha quality which helps and serves all sentient beings is the Form Body, not the Truth Body. So when Bodhisattvas cultivate the genuine aspiration to achieve enlightenment, they concentrate mainly on achieving the Form Body.

In order to achieve the resultant Form Body, one has to accumulate the necessary causes and conditions according to the laws of cause and effect which pervade all impermanent phenomena, including the Buddha state. One has to gather a substantial cause for this Form

Body, which the practice of wisdom cannot become. Achievement of the Form Body is like the resultant imprint of accumulated merit.

Although according to the sutras the practices of generosity, discipline and so forth can also be causes for the Form Body, they cannot be its substantial cause. The factor which serves as the complete, substantial cause for the Form Body is the one practiced in tantra. This refers to the special energy, the winds.

On the other hand, wisdom realizing emptiness is a substantial cause for the achievement of the Truth Body.

Since there are two types of resultant bodies, there are also two different causes. If the special energy, the winds, is not generated together with wisdom, then there cannot be the combination of method and wisdom.

Therefore one should develop a type of mind which, although of one entity, has both the aspect of method and the aspect of wisdom for the actualization of both the Form Body and the Truth Body, complete within the entity of one mind.

Generally if we ask what the Form Body looks like, then there is not a definite answer. One cannot say it looks like a statue. But one can at least have an idea of something which can be imagined by human beings of this world.

One should take the object of such a form, a divinity which has features similar to the resultant Form Body; and, focussing on such a form, reflect on its emptiness.

Here we have the appearance of the deity and at the same time an understanding of its empty nature. Therefore such a mind has both of these qualities, the visualization of the deity and also the understanding of emptiness complete in it.

For this reason it is useful to visualize deities and mandalas in tantric practice.

Question: Your Holiness, when we enter the temple, there is an inscription saying that "All existence is like a reflection, clear and pure, without turbulence, it cannot be grasped and it cannot be expressed, without self-nature, without location, perfectly established by way of their causes and action." Could you please explain this inscription?

His Holiness: It says in the first line that, speaking from the viewpoint of ordinary consciousnesses like ours, all phenomena are like reflections. Although they appear in one way, they exist in another; they appear as truly existent, but they do not exist truly. Therefore there is a contradiction, just as a reflection of a face appears in a mirror as if it were the face itself, but is not the face.

In the second line three factors are mentioned: clear, pure, and without turbulence. These refer to the three objects of abandonment: obscuration of delusions; obscuration to knowledge; and obscuration to absorption, or the meditative state. The line says that by understanding the nature of non-inherent existence to the fullest extent, one is freed from these three types of obscurations.

The third line that existence "cannot be grasped and it cannot be expressed" means that the experience of realization cannot be grasped by someone like ourselves through our conceptual thought, nor can it be expressed fully through conventional words.

The last line, "without self-nature, without location, perfectly established by way of their causes and action", refers to the three doors of liberation.

Question: If a phenomenon as we understand it is the designation of our consciousness, is the phenomenon purely a mental construction?

His Holiness: Although it is the case that phenomena are imputed by conceptual thought, nothing can exist just by being labelled. It is not the case that anything that is imputed by a consciousness becomes that imputed object; phenomena cannot be manipulated as the consciousness wishes.

If that were the case, that consciousness, conceptual thought, could do what it wanted. There would be no difference between valid and invalid cognition, or between right and wrong.

Since phenomena do exist, but their true existence has been refuted logically, the only choice left is that they exist nominally, through designation. But this does not mean that anything we designate would become our designation of it.

In his *Fundamental Treatise of Wisdom* Nagarjuna refutes the assertion that Lord Buddha cannot be omniscient because he did not answer certain questions. Nagarjuna explains that Buddha's not answering those questions proves instead his omniscience.

This implies that when if there is no use for words it is better not to speak at all. Whatever is said should be beneficial.

One of the ten non-virtuous actions is called derisive talk. When we talk to divide friends, then even if we tell the truth we create a non-virtuous action. One has to avoid this. When talk is helpful, then even lying can be a virtuous action. Everything depends on whether talk benefits or not.

In certain teachings Lord Buddha said that the five aggregates are like the load, and that the person is like the carrier of the load. Here he has explained the self as something substantially existent. This really contradicts the ultimate viewpoint of the Buddha himself.

He made this statement to benefit people who adhered very strongly to the view of a self. If he had said to those people that there is no self, they might have concluded that nothing at all matters.

Question: Your Holiness, is reason of ultimate value?

His Holiness: Some types of phenomenon can be approached by our conventional level of intelligence, but there are other types of phenomena that we are not able to perceive or approach unless our states of mind are heightened. Even such higher states still adhere to the law of clear thinking.

In Mahayana Buddhism, one direct assumption is that there are two types of teachings of the Buddha: definitive and interpretive. Some of the Buddha's teachings can be taken at their face value, but others cannot be taken literally.

How do we determine what can be taken literally? This can be decided only through logical reasoning, because Buddha's words are expressed differently in different contexts. To avoid endless speculation we decide finally through logical reasoning.

The position which cannot be contradicted by reasoning is the ultimate viewpoint of the Buddha.

Question: Your Holiness, in tantric meditation we must visualize our enemies in front of us. As we consider our main enemies to be delusions, is it wise to keep our delusions in front of us?

His Holiness: We have to agree that conventionally there exist different kinds of people like friends and enemies. While there might be situations in which our perception of someone as an enemy might be mistaken because of not knowing his motivation conventionally, we can agree that there are different classes of people, such as friends and enemies.

Should we talk of an enemy who will always be an enemy from the beginning to the end, then the real enemy is delusion. But this does not negate the external enemy, the being as a person.

Since there are enemies who intend to harm us, they should be seen as the objects of patience, the basis upon which we cultivate patience. If we tried to cultivate patience by focusing on our own delusions, then we would gain nothing. What we are concerned with here is to eliminate the experience of hatred and desire that arises just because someone is in the role of an enemy or a friend, to stop that kind of fluctuating emotion based on delusion.

In order to fight the inner enemy, the first Buddhist step is on the defensive level, the second on the offensive level.

Since in the first phase of training we are not in a position to defeat delusions, we employ defensive tactics so as not to fall under the influence of more delusions. The immediate practice in which a layman can engage is to restrain his physical and verbal actions from the ten non-virtuous actions, such as killing, stealing and so forth. This is the immediate practice.

Generally speaking, everybody regards killing as bad, and often the legal punishment for it is the death sentence. Everybody also agrees that stealing is bad.

A practitioner of the Buddhadharma, whether there is a policeman present or not, should always be able to observe pure discipline on his own, refraining from killing and stealing. A practitioner has his own police force within himself; he is always alert, always examining to see whether he is doing right or wrong, whether his motivation is pure or not.

It is effective to start the day with something like a mental master-plan. As soon as you wake up in the morning, tell yourself, "Generally until my death, but particularly this month—this very day—I shall lead a spiritual life. At least I shall not engage in anything that brings harm to others, and I will try to help them."

If you are in business, engineering or educational work, or in any professional field, observe high principles.

Even in warfare this is important. If you have to kill in warfare, do it with high principles, and do not lose human feeling. Do it only when absolutely necessary.

In modern warfare, human feeling diminishes as actions are mechanized. Machines have no mercy, so naturally wars become very destructive. Women and children are killed because the bomb has no conscience, no discrimination.

I really think that we put too much emphasis on machines. In fields such as construction they are all right, but not in other fields. We should lead our daily lives with principle.

The police force, intelligence agency, and supreme court must be within ourselves. Be your own policeman and judge. If you do something wrong, punish yourself, not physically but mentally. Regret and acknowledge the mistake.

Then later in the evening before you go to sleep, do not calculate just the profit and loss of money. It is also important to calculate your mental activities during the day. Ask yourself how many negative mental activities happened, and how many positive mental activities.

Because you give this subject special attention, as time goes by your behaviour will improve. A person who is easily irritated will become more gentle. That is the first level of practice. Once you gain inner strength and self-discipline to control misbehaviour and become a good and honest being, a warm-hearted person who does not harm others, one with more compassion, more love, more kindness as these qualities increase you will become more stable. You also will become more courageous, and your willpower will increase. These are good human qualities.

Usually I tell people that compassion, warm-heartedness, is something we can call universal religion. It is valid whether we believe in reincarnation or not, believe in a God or not, whether we believe in Buddha or not.

Specific belief is something different; the most important is to be a good human being. Sooner or later we have to die, and if then we review the past years with regret, it is too late, isn't it?

Spend each day of your life in a useful way. Try not to harm others, and instead to help them. Then when the final day comes, you will be happy, satisfied. Though some of your friends may cry, you will have no regrets. If as a Buddhist you cultivated good seeds in this lifetime, you have the guarantee that your next life will be a better one.

Eventually we should begin to think more about emptiness. That is the starting point to take up the offensive against the inner enemy. Here, too, ultimately the main factor is your own motivation.

I think it was former Prime Minister Morarji Desai who told me, as we discussed non-violence, that method is most important. Despite good motivation and good results, violence is always bad. This was his attitude.

Yet from the Buddhist's viewpoint, motivation and result are more important than means. If one's motivation is good, the end is good. When your motivation and aim are good, but the result is not a good one, then motivation is more important. Despite a lack of success, if your motivation was sincere, there is no defect.

There is a story from Tibet. A statue of the Buddha was outside in the rain. A person passing saw the statue and thought, "Rain should not fall on an image of the Buddha." So he looked around for something to cover it with. He could find nothing other than a pair of soles of old shoes, so he covered the statue of the Buddha with those soles.

Another person passed by and thought, "How can anyone place old soles on a statue of the Buddha?" He removed the shoes. Because in both cases the motivation was sincere, there was no harm done. Both generated equal positive karma.

We have been discussing how to manage our minds, how to purify and improve them. This is something very important. It is at the beginning difficult to practise. But make constant effort, and as time goes by, your experience will improve.

4

Buddhist Perspectives

Vajrapani, Bodhisattva of Power

Integrating Practice

At this time, when violence and cruelty are increasing, Buddha's message of non-violence is very important.

Like Mahatma Gandhi, I feel that the essence of the teachings of Buddha and many other ancient Indian teachers should be implemented in the field of daily life. Take the essence and apply it to your professional life; that is the proper way. If we regard religious and spiritual teachings as something in isolation, then they are of little use. And if in our worldly lives we forget about spiritual practice, that is not right either.

I feel that while India is developing materially through science and technology, it is extremely important to preserve her rich cultural heritages. If at some time in the future the world population lives in harmony, and on a genuine, voluntary basis all of humanity becomes almost like one family, without any differences and conflicts, then that oneness is all right. If such a good day comes then we can let go of our cultural heritages, which give us a separate identity.

Meanwhile, I think that to preserve one's own cultural heritage is important. This is especially true in the case of the ancient cultural heritage of India, which is so closely related to mental development. Material progress should go together with culture, which is very closely related to mental development.

As I mentioned earlier, this meeting is completely informal. You should feel as if we have gathered in your own home and we are exchanging experiences and discussing ideas about ways and means to minimize our daily problems and increase our mental peace and goodness. If we have mental peace, then there will be a more peaceful atmosphere in our own house, and this will help future generations, our children and grandchildren.

The Four Noble Truths and Dependent Arising

When we have problems one way to cope, at least on a temporary basis, is simply to forget them. When your mind is exhausted and has become heavy, go away for a weekend or take a few days' holiday

That is one method, but a very temporary one. The problem remains.

Another way to relieve the problem is to look at it and analyze it. When you look at it from a very close range, then it appears very big, like something unbearable; but when you look at the same problem from a distance, then it becomes smaller. Analyze the problem; think about it. That is very useful.

When Buddha, before he entered the spiritual path, saw the terrible suffering of human beings, he knew that suffering was an undesirable phenomenon, and he searched for methods and means to overcome it.

In the course of his search, before he achieved enlightenment, Buddha Shakyamuni undertook the strictest trainings. For example, he meditated for six years, eating hardly any food. This is of great significance because it shows that for religious practice one must have great courage and one must be prepared to endure severe hardships.

This is also illustrated by the lives of many great masters of different traditions. Many of them underwent sacrifices for their spiritual purification.

The first teaching Buddha gave after his enlightenment was that of the Four Noble Truths. These are explained on the basis of cause and effect.

That which is known as cyclic existence, or samsara, is the cause of undesirable sufferings as a consequence of negative actions. Nirvana or liberation is the effect of having transcended these negative patterns. In order to explain cyclic existence and the force by which a person is propelled into it, the Buddha taught the first Two Noble Truths: the truth of suffering and the truth of the cause of suffering. Then he taught the second Two Noble Truths: the state of nirvana or liberation, which is known as the state of ultimate peace or cessation of suffering; and the path to that cessation. The cause that brings about such a realization is called the truth of the path to cessation.

Therefore the Buddha first identified the Four Noble Truths by saying. "This is the truth of suffering; this is the truth of its source; this is the truth of cessation; and this is the truth of the path which leads to it."

With the identification of the Four Noble Truths, the Buddha presented the actual way we arrive at an understanding of them.

In order to explain how the understanding of these Four Noble Truths is to be incorporated into one's own practice of the spiritual path, the Buddha taught that suffering is something that has to be recognized and that the source of suffering is something that has to be abandoned. Until we recognize that suffering is dangerous, we will make no attempt to get rid of it. So first we recognize that the very presence of cyclic existence is suffering. Realizing that cyclic existence, the source of suffering, is something one has to transcend, and that cessation is something that one has to achieve, we follow the path to cessation. We must meditate on this path in order to achieve cessation.

Analysis of suffering leads us into apparent contradiction, as expressed in the Buddha's statements: "Suffering is to be recognized, but there is no suffering that can be recognized; the source of suffering is to be abandoned, but there is nothing to be abandoned; cessation is to be achieved, but there is nothing to be achieved; the path to cessation is something to be meditated on, but there is nothing to be meditated on."

Contradictions arise because looking at suffering and analyzing it, we do not find suffering as something independently or objectively or truly existing in its own right. Rather, both the undesirable experience of suffering and the desirable phenomenon of ultimate happiness, ultimate peace, nirvana, are products of causes and conditions. No independent thing exists; everything depends on a cause.

Buddha gave a more detailed explanation of suffering, the cause of suffering, and how suffering develops from causes in his teachings of the twelve links of dependent origination or arising.

The twelve links are: ignorance; karmic formation; consciousnesses; name and form; six entrances or sources; contact; feeling; desire or craving; attachment or grasping; imprint or becoming; birth; and aging and death.

The implication of dependent origination is that each stage depends on a previous stage and will not arise without it. In order to stop aging and death, we have to stop the actual troublemaker, the stage we do not want, which is samsaric rebirth produced from the contaminated forces of karma and delusion.

For that, we have to achieve cessation of ignorance. If we stop the first stage, then the other eleven cease automatically.

The process of how suffering arises was explained by the Indian master Asanga on the basis of what is known as the three conditions.

The first condition is immovability. Immovability means that sufferings are produced by an intention, not by someone like a creator, and they exist as a result of their own causes.

The second is the condition of impermanence. This means that although sufferings arise from their own causes and conditions, these causes and conditions have to be impermanent because permanent phenomena cannot produce effects.

The third condition is known as that of having a specific potential. Saying that causes and conditions are impermanent is not enough; what is necessary is that each cause and condition should show its unique potential to produce an individual effect. A certain condition cannot produce just anything.

Buddha identified the cause as ignorance.

Buddhists do not accept a creator. They prefer to think of self-creation. Ultimately, the creator is one's own mind. As long as one's mind is impure, the result is negative; unwanted results will follow. But once one's mind is purified, enlightened, then all negative results have ceased, and positive results follow.

Sometimes I tell my friends that Buddhism is a human religion and has nothing to do with God. It mainly deals with how to behave oneself and how to train one's own mind.

But this does not mean that Buddhists do not accept higher beings. From the point of view of experienced or enlightened higher beings, there is not only one God, there are thousands, millions of gods, such as *devas*. We accept that.

Especially in the Tantrayana there are many deities, wrathful deities as well as peaceful deities. All these deities, gods and goddesses, *devas* and *devis*, are manifestations of one being, or in some cases just the creation of one's own mind.

More importantly to all Buddhists, Buddha Shakyamuni was an experienced teacher, full of compassion and wisdom, who through his own experiences showed us ways and means to purify our own mind. Buddha Shakyamuni achieved enlightenment through the hard process of his spiritual practices.

Buddha himself explained the actual arising of the twelve links of interdependent origination, from ignorance to the twelfth, aging and death, and he also explained the way through which one can end this process.

Having explained how one goes through this cycle of existence and also how to stop it on the basis of the Four Noble Truths, the Buddha then explained what is known as the two truths.

When he says that suffering is something to be recognized, but there is nothing to be recognized, that statement actually shows the two truths. On a relative level there is one aspect, and on the ultimate level there is another.

For example, you see this beautiful flower. It is changing all the time, and when it is exposed to high temperatures it will change even more. We see the effect that conditions like heat or cold have on the changing of the flower.

Someone may say, "This rose is very good, good scent, good colour." However, someone else may say, "Oh, this rose is not good. It looks beautiful, but it is very thorny. When I touch it, it hurts me."

So, here we have one object seen from different angles, as good, bad, or neutral. Because its nature is relative, we can explain it indifferent ways. This shows that it depends on other factors. If something that is beautiful or of good or bad quality were independent, then it would not matter from what angle one looked at it. It would always remain beautiful or good or bad; it would remain independent.

This shows that the concept, in this case of beauty, is relative. When we look at a common object like this flower from different angles and also at the concepts which are produced from these different angles, then it occurs to us that there must be something on the basis of this object that allows all these different concepts. The absence of independent nature acts as this basis.

When the table is empty we can put many things on it, but when it is already occupied then there is no space for more things. Ultimate nature acts as the basis for receiving things or enabling them to have all their different functions.

This shows that there exists two levels. On one level, all these different aspects can work on certain bases. These bases we cannot see directly, but when we think deeply we can feel that there is something that makes all these aspects possible.

These two truths, relative and ultimate, are different phenomenon. Understanding them helps in our understanding of the Four Noble Truths.

The truth of the cause of suffering is explained on the basis of what is known as the two sources: delusions and the karmic actions which are motivated by delusions.

Buddha said that delusions themselves are the product of an undisciplined, negative state of mind, but this undisciplined state of mind itself depends very much on causes and conditions.

As explained earlier, since these different aspects of the mind also depend on causes and conditions, this mind has a certain nature which makes it possible for it to transform into different states, like positive and negative. There is, therefore, a possibility to eliminate these delusions, these preconceptions which are products of causes and conditions.

This is how we establish that cessation of suffering exists. It is through the understanding of these two truths that we come to fully understand the Four Noble Truths.

The Four Noble Truths are elaborately explained in both Hinayana and Mahayana literature, but we can find elaborate explanations of the two truths only in Mahayana.

Through the understanding of the two truths, one comes to understand the Four Noble Truths; and through the understanding of the Four Noble Truths, one comes to understand the Three Jewels: the Buddha, the Dharma, and the Sangha.

The person who reaches the highest state of purification, elimination of all negative thought, is a Buddha; and those who are in the process of purification comprise the Sangha. All the good qualities of the mind we call Dharma.

Hinayana, Mahayana, Tantrayana

The methods of achieving cessation are explained in the three higher trainings of the Hinayana tradition.

The first higher training is that of wisdom, the actual weapon that destroys ignorance.

In order to enable the practitioner to use this weapon of wisdom in a strong and effective way, the training of concentration, single-pointedness of mind is explained.

It in turn is based on the training of self-discipline.

The best method, according to the Mahayana, is for the practitioner to be inspired by the motivation of spiritual altruism. That is, on the bases of compassion for other beings, and the aspiration to achieve enlightenment for their sake, the practitioner engages in the practice of the six perfections: generosity, discipline, patience, enthusiastic perseverance, concentration and wisdom.

Another higher or more sophisticated method is explained in the tantric vehicle. In order to speed up the achievement of enlightenment, one employs certain yogas whereby the practitioner actually prevents the appearance and conception of himself as an ordinary being and generates himself into a deity, a divine form and then engages in the practice. That is the tantric method.

Within Tantrayana, we also practice the path of the highest yoga tantra. The main aspects of this practice are method and wisdom.

Although method and wisdom have many different meanings according to different contexts, what is meant by wisdom here is the consciousness that realizes the nature of emptiness. Method is the aspiration to achieve enlightenment for the sake of all sentient beings. The actual practice of these two factors should be undertaken on the basis of one's own mental meditation.

One can do so without any visualization of divine objects, but it helps to take a divine being as an object for the practice. Therefore, according to this text (taught in Part B of Chapter Three), we visualize five divine beings.

Since here we are meditating on deities, there is also a part where one recites the mantras of the particular deities, but the actual practices should be done through mental meditation. However, when one feels tired at the end of the meditation session, instead of giving work to the mind, one can give work to the mouth and recite mantras.

Correct Environment

The first paragraph of the text (see *Appendix*) explains the environment in which the practice is to be undertaken.

For the beginner, the place is quite important. Once we have developed certain experiences, then external factors have very little effect. But generally speaking, the place for meditation should be quiet.

When we meditate on single-pointedness of mind, then we need a completely isolated place, one with no noise. That is very important. Then for certain yoga practices, the altitude also makes a difference. A higher altitude is better; high mountains are the best place.

Also, there are sites where experienced meditators have lived before, and thus blessed and empowered the place. So later, persons of less experience are inspired by the place, get vibrations or blessings from the place. First one highly developed person blesses the place, and later these blessings are transmitted to other meditators.

When we clean and tidy up the room our wish should not be just to have a clean place, but to put our minds in order. When later we visualize deities, make offerings, and recite mantras, it is as if we had prepared to receive important guests. When we expect an invited guest, then first we clean and tidy up. It is not nice to invite a guest into an untidy place. In order to practice meditation, first clean your room. Your wish to do so should not be polluted by negative states of mind like attachment, aversion or similar attitudes.

There is a story about one of the great meditators in Tibet. One day he arranged his offerings particularly well, then he sat down and thought, "Why did I do that?"

He realized that he had done it because he wanted to impress one of his benefactors, who was going to come and see him on that day. He was so disgusted with his polluted motivation that he took a handful of dust and threw it over the offerings.

This meditator had once been a thief. Occasionally he would still be moved by the urge to steal. When once he visited a certain family, his right hand automatically reached out toward a beautiful object. With his left hand he caught it and called out, "Here is a thief, here is a thief." He could train himself in this way. This was really a very effective way of practicing, because at every moment he implemented the right thing.

Similarly, when we clean or make some preparations, our motivation must be pure and sincere. Worldly concerns should be involved as little as possible.

Then the way in which the different objects of refuge should be arranged on the altar is explained (in the text). If you can afford to have all the required religious objects, then you should display them. If you cannot afford them, then no matter. The great meditator of Tibet, the yogi Milarepa, had nothing apart from some rolls of paper which contained instructions by his master Marpa, which he put up around the cave. He did not have anything in his cave, but one night a thief broke in. Milarepa laughed and said, "Since I cannot find anything here during the day, what is there that you will find during the night?" It is said that a real meditator never feels the lack of external materials.

Symbols of Refuge

First the statue of the Buddha is explained.

The Sanskrit term 'Buddha' indicates a being whose mind is purified of faults and whose realizations have completely developed.

Buddha is also known as Tathagatha, the one who has entered into the nature of suchness and the one who arose from it.

When one explains the meaning of someone arising from the nature of suchness then one comes to the topic of the three bodies of a Buddha: Truth Body (*Dharmakaya*), Enjoyment Body (*Sambhogakaya*), and Emanation Body (*Nirmanakaya*)

Detailed explanations of the three bodies of the Buddhas can be found throughout Mahayana literature.

According to this doctrine, when the Buddha came into this universe as Buddha Shakyamuni he assumed the Emanation Body from the Truth Body. Here all the great events in the life of the Buddha, starting from conception in the womb up to his *Parinirvana*, are regarded as deeds of the Buddha.

The Buddhas are also known as Gone to Bliss (*Sugata*), the ones who have passed into peace, the ones who have traveled the peaceful path into a peaceful state. This term includes peaceful realizations, peaceful abandonments or cessation, and the Buddha nature, the essence of Buddha that, according to Buddhist doctrine, is inherent in all sentient beings.

Generally the body, speech and mind of the Buddhas are explained as having different manifestations: the body as Avalokiteshvara, speech as Manjushri, and mind as Vajrapani. But in the text (see *Appendix*) you will find Avalokiteshvara, Manjushri, and Vajrapani explained as the embodiments of compassion, wisdom, and energy of the Buddhas.

Avalokiteshvara and Manjushri appear as peaceful deities, whereas Vajrapani appears slightly wrathful.

Generally speaking, when someone has strong force of mind he can engage in actions more drastically and more forcefully, and this is the reason for having wrathful deities. According to highest yoga tantra, one calls this "taking desire or anger into the path."

Here Tara, another peaceful deity is spoken of as the purifying aspect of the energy of the body. All the different qualities of the

Buddha, including compassion, wisdom and power, depend on the moving factor, which is energy.

One can also say that Tara is the feminist deity. There is a legend according to which Tara, when she cultivated the aspiration to achieve enlightenment, made it a point to become enlightened in her female form.

As a representation of the speech of the Buddhas, we use a sacred text, if possible a copy of the *Perfection of Wisdom Sutra* or *Prajnaparamita Sutra*

Prajnaparamita means the wisdom gone beyond. There are different types of wisdom, such as natural wisdom, the path which leads to it, and the resultant wisdom state. The *Perfection of Wisdom* explains these different types of wisdom.

This type of literature constitutes the main body of Mahayana scripture. In the Tibetan translation of the sacred Buddhist canon there are some twenty volumes of *The Perfection of Wisdom Sutras*, comprised of about twenty different texts. The most extensive text has one hundred thousand verses, the next twenty-five thousand, eight thousand, and so forth.

The shortest text consists of the letter *Ah*. This is known as the *Perfection of Wisdom Sutra* of one letter. In Sanskrit, *Ah* is the letter for negation because suchness, or the ultimate nature, as we already discussed, is the absence of independent existence; this is a negation.

The next symbol of refuge is the stupa. This represents the mind of the Buddhas. There exist eight different types of stupas, for example, those symbolizing victory over demons, enlightenment, *Parinirvana*, and so forth. When I look at these different kinds of stupas, I think that they were developed as a means of remembrance.

Next the offering of pure water, flowers, incense, light, and fruit is placed on the altar. This is modeled on the custom of how a guest was served in India at the time. If Buddha had taught Buddhism in Tibet he would have talked about offerings like butter and *tsampa*.

Physical Posture and Breathing

Next I will explain the physical posture during meditation. The meditation seat should be slightly raised at the back because that helps reduce tightness. The present seat on which I am sitting is springy; the front is actually higher than the back, just the opposite.

Sitting in vajra (cross-legged) position is very difficult, but if it causes no pain then that is the proper way. Or you can sit in half vajra (His Holiness demonstrated a very comfortable cross-legged position), or in Arya Tara's posture (again demonstrated), which is very comfortable.

In the correct hand mudra, the back of the right hand rests in the palm of the left hand and the two thumbs stand up and touch one another, forming a triangle. This triangle has a tantric significance, symbolizing the Realm of Truth (*Dharmadhatu*), the reality source and also inner heat at the navel.

The arms should not touch the body. The head is slightly bent down, the tip of the tongue touching the palate, which prevents thirst and drooling when the meditator engages in deep, single-pointed concentration. Lips and teeth should be left in their natural position, eyes looking at the tip of the nose. This is no problem when one has a big, pointed nose, but when one has a small nose, looking at its tip sometimes causes pain. (Laughing.) So this depends on the size of one's nose.

As to the position of the eyes, at the beginning it might give you a clearer visualization when they are closed, but in the long run this is not good; you should not close your eyes. Visualization is done on a mental and not a sensory level. If you train yourself to meditate with open eyes and become used to it, then even when an object comes in front of your eyes, you will not lose the mental image you are meditating on. On the other hand, if you train yourself and become used to meditating with closed eyes, you will lose the mental image the moment you open them.

During meditation your breathing should be natural. You should not breathe violently nor too gently. Sometimes if you are meditating in connection with tantric practices and do certain energy yogas, like the nine-round breathing practice, then it is different.

When you are in a fluctuating state of mind, like when you are angry or have lost your temper, then it is good to bring back calmness by concentrating on breathing. Just count the breaths, completely forgetting about anger. Concentrate on breathing and count in/out "one, two, three," up to twenty.

At that moment when your mind concentrates fully on breathing, the breath coming and going, the passions subside. Afterwards it is easier to think clearly.

Since all activities, including meditation, depend very much on the force of intention or motivation, it is important that, before you begin to meditate, you cultivate a correct motivation. We are engaged here in a practice which is connected with tantra, so the appropriate motivation is to avoid being distracted by concern for this life alone. Nor should our motivation be influenced by concern for perfection and happiness of samsaric life alone.

The correct motivation is the altruistic attitude.

Questions and Answers

Question: Is it possible to go directly, just by pure meditation of the mind and without the complexities of the stepping-stones of deities?

His Holiness: One aspect of the nature of mind is colourless, formless. Yet it is some kind of entity which has the quality of reflecting opposites.

We can neither hold nor imagine this entity. Just as form reflects in a clear mirror, when the form that appears in the mirror is taken away, its reflection in the mirror has vanished as well.

It is the same with the mind; it reflects the object. This is one level, one nature of the mind.

For such meditation there is no need for devotion. Just concentrate on it daily; it will improve. But here the subject is the mind of enlightenment, a special kind of altruism, one linked to the understanding of emptiness.

This also prepares one for deity yoga. Once one has received an initiation, the actual practice of Tantrayana is deity yoga. One visualizes oneself as deities, and this makes a foundation for deity yoga.

In order to reach this spontaneous and unsimulated yoga, one has to go through the process of the simulated and artificial stages. Therefore Buddha has explained in tantra that simulated or artificial yoga is the boat by which one crosses the river. The purpose of getting into the boat is not just to travel in it, but rather you are using it as a means to cross over to the other shore.

Once you have reached the shore of spontaneous yoga, then you leave behind the artificial.

In this connection, one of the Tibetan masters said that although it is the case that sooner or later you have to abandon the boat, the time of abandoning it is when you have reached the other side, not on this side.

I think, according to a Tibetan tradition, that when you start to investigate directly, without deity yoga, seeking some kind of direct experience of purity of consciousness, you use conceptual thought. This has its limitations as a method.

The proper way is without disturbance of mind, of basic consciousness, to apply some kind of simultaneity, exceptional experience.

That is very difficult. When we say it 'direct approach' it seems very easy, very powerful, doesn't it? But the actual experience is quite difficult.

To some of my friends who are still alive, that experience occasionally occurred. In those strong or very clear moments, one remembers events of past lives; not of one life but of hundreds of lifetimes. When these memories come up, some kind of very subtle consciousness becomes evident. Those types of people do have some fleeting moments of experiences of the subtlest state of mind, during which it is possible to recollect experiences of past lives.

Sometimes such states of mind occur after great devotion, for example, after many years of practicing one hundred thousand prostrations, one hundred thousand mandalas, or one hundred thousand recitations of the hundred-syllable mantra.

This is very hard work, a rigorous practice. But sometimes it induces spontaneous experiences.

Question: Your Holiness, I would like to begin with what you said earlier, that the teaching of Buddhism is like a treasure which came from India to Tibet, and that Tibet preserved it. I think that we Indians have been very unfortunate to have let it go away from our country because we did not appreciate the treasure that it was.

Firstly I think we have to be ready enough to receive it. I would like to make this point.

Secondly, you mentioned the twelve various intermediate states, ignorance, and the rest. When the point of nirvana comes, there is complete cessation of suffering, no birth. Only a very few people reach that stage. But people like us, millions of us, who experience cyclic existence and who are householders and who work, even if we try to achieve at least some of the qualities you mentioned, we have to be in touch with all kinds of people and situations all the time, some of which are under control but most of which are not. How would you guide us common householders?

His Holiness: I know what you mean from my own experience, and also from the experiences of friends who have gone through difficult circumstances.

First you acquire a knowledge of the nature of cyclic existence and nirvana, and the possibility of and methods for achieving nirvana.

You may not be able to implement them all at the present moment. Take my own case, for example. In my situation it is difficult to perform certain practices like *shamata* meditation. For the practice of *shamata* we need to live in complete isolation, in a remote place, for at least a few years. Otherwise it is impossible to achieve the results. Under the present circumstances it is impossible for the Dalai Lama to practice like that.

But knowledge or some kind of understanding about the nature of cyclic existence, the nature of human life, is of great help. When we face our own problems or the problems of others, we can understand those as being due to the basic nature of cyclic existence. They become something natural.

Every human action, whether good or bad, is based on motivation. Sometimes we face circumstances that make us angry or frustrated. But once we have gained some understanding of cyclic existence, then in similar circumstances we become able to control or at least minimize negative thought. As a result our mind will not lose peace.

If we have a proper understanding of the path, the actual resultant stage, and the method which leads to it, then even though we cannot implement the practice during our daily life, this understanding will serve as the background which helps us to face day-to-day difficulties.

A householder, as compared to a monk, has more work to do. You have to look after your husband or your wife, or your children. When you have grandchildren you have even more people to look after.

Here motivation is most important. In actual life you sometimes have to say some harsh words or you have to take strong action in order to protect them, in order to benefit them. The key point is motivation. The same action done with sincere and good motivation is sincere and good.

For example, there are two people, and an enemy is going to hurt or kill them. Both take counteractions in order to protect themselves.

Both take the same action, but one of them does so with a selfish motivation, without thinking of the enemy's side, and through that way he feels strong hatred for the enemy. He takes counteraction with that motivation.

The other person commits the same counteraction but with the motivation that, "If I allow this person to kill me or whatever he wants to do, the ultimate result is that he will collect negative karma and he will suffer."

Temporarily he may feel satisfied, but ultimately he will suffer, won't he? If we take counteraction in order to save the enemy from wrong doing, then the same action is very different due to the motivation.

For example, when the Chinese invaded Tibet, we were trying to fight them. The motivation was that we sincerely respect the Chinese as human beings just like us who want happiness and not suffering, but we also take certain actions to protect ourselves in order to stop the Chinese from wrongdoing, without losing respect and compassion in thought.

Question: In the discussion of the higher state of consciousness as presented in the Greater Vehicle, there is talk about relative reality and ultimate reality.

These are not really two different things, are they?

His Holiness: The two truths are an explanation of one object looked at from two different angles. Since the two truths are explained on the basis of one object they are actually of one entity, but they are also regarded as mutually exclusive.

Let us take the example of a person who is very learned, a very able person but also very cunning. We want to employ that person according to his ability, but that person is not trustworthy. So from that angle we have to take other measures, to be careful. Although we deal with the same person, we confront a contradiction, his two aspects; one is very negative, the other very positive.

In our case, we do not have a negative and a positive aspect, but there is a similarity in how the two truths manifest within one object.

Take this flower, for example. It has a relative level of existence, where all the conventions operate, like colour and scent. Then there is the deeper, ultimate reality.

This is like looking at one object from two sides. Because of dependent arising, phenomena lack inherent existence. Since phenomena lack inherent or true existence, since they originate dependently, they are also deeply interconnected. Even the understanding of the two is interconnected.

The division into the two vehicles of Mahayana and Hinayana is made on the basis of the depths of the motivation. As the Mahayana motivation is more encompassing, the resultant state is also explained as being more encompassing.

There are some texts which say that at the ordinary level sentient beings do have different entities, that they are different beings, but that ultimately, when they become enlightened, they all become one, absorbed into one wisdom-ocean. Water coming from different rivers has different colours, tastes and speeds; but when it merges with the infinite ocean it loses its identity and becomes of one taste and colour.

This does not mean that when a person reaches Buddhahood his own personal identity is no more. It is not like that. He reaches the same kind of rank, yet the individual self or I is still there.

Question: Your Holiness, when you talked about the scripture with the many verses, the shortest just the letter *Ah*, which means negative, does it mean that in the whole philosophy, first comes the negative, and from that one rises to various kinds of dialectical positions?

His Holiness: When I said that *Ah* actually explained emptiness, I did not mean to say that emptiness is very sacred, but rather that this letter *Ah* is very sacred.

Emptiness happens to be a phenomenon which is negative. Negative phenomenon means here that when we perceive or recognize it, we have to do so by explicitly negating its opposite factor. That type of phenomenon is known as a negative phenomenon.

For example, let us talk about the absence of an elephant. In order to realize the absence of an elephant, first of all we have to identify what is to be negated, i.e., elephant. Then through explicitly negating the existence of elephant we realize the absence of elephant. Phenomena are divided into two categories: negative and affirmative. Negative phenomena are further divided into two: mere negation of the opposite factor, which is known as non-affirmative negative; and affirmative negative phenomena.

For example, is this flower a rose or a tulip? This is not a tulip. Although this is a negative statement, it affirms something. It suggests something implicitly, whereas in the case of the absence of an elephant, apart from negating the presence of an elephant, it does not affirm or suggest anything implicitly.

In the same way, emptiness is a negative phenomenon, the mere absence or mere negation of inherent or true existence. The syllable *Ah* explains emptiness because *Ah* is a term of negation.

One can also say that because things lack inherent or true existence, functions like cause and effect become possible. Therefore one can say that conventional realities arise from the nature of emptiness.

5

Discovering Wisdom

Tara, Bodhisattva of Enlightenment Activity

Motivation

The best type of motivation is the *bodhichitta*, the intention to achieve enlightenment for the sake of other sentient beings. The next best motivation is that we should at least have the aspiration to achieve liberation. And the third type of motivation is that we should be free from attachment to the affairs of this lifetime, and aim instead for happiness for all future lives.

In order to cultivate the appropriate or correct motivation, reflect that this life which we hold so dear passes quickly. If it were something durable, something eternal, then it would be worthwhile holding it dear. But our lifetime is limited to a maximum of a hundred years, in some rare cases to one hundred and twenty, one hundred and thirty years. It is impossible for an ordinary human being to live beyond that. Always remember impermanence.

It is a well-known fact that when the phenomenon called death occurs, things like wealth, fame, and power accumulated in this lifetime cannot help us.

Life itself is a phenomenon that changes momentarily. If someone totally neglects to provide for future lives and is too much preoccupied with the concerns of this life alone, in his eagerness to have a good time in this life he grasps too much or has too great an attachment. In the end he will face many more problems.

Right from the beginning our attitude towards this life should be well-balanced, should reflect a somewhat relaxed attitude. Then when things become difficult, the depth of mental disturbance will be limited.

Sometimes it is very helpful to read biographies of those people who have more experience of life than ourselves. We should contemplate the fact that, when people are too much preoccupied with the affairs of this life, they face more adverse circumstances. On the other hand when people adopt a rational and more realistic approach to life, they have fewer troubles and difficulties.

Then there is the question of whether there is a next life or not. This is a key point. There are people even today who have very clear memories of their past lives.

The rational premise which establishes past and future lifetimes is the factor of the different causes of mind and matter.

Both mind and matter depend on their causes and conditions; this is proven by the fact that they are subject to change.

There are two types of causes: substantial causes and co-operative causes. Just as matter requires a substantial cause which has its identical continuity, which is matter, so consciousness is produced from an earlier moment of consciousness, the continuity of which is produced from a substantial cause, which is an earlier moment of itself.

Consciousness

Consciousnesses are generally divided into two: sensory consciousnesses and mental consciousnesses. The rise of a sensory consciousness, such as eye-consciousness, depends on certain conditions, including the objective condition and the internal condition, which is the empowering condition.

On the basis of these two conditions, the eye-consciousness also requires another factor, the preceding moment of the consciousness itself.

Let us talk about the basis of this flower and the eye-consciousness which sees it. The function of the objective condition, which is the flower, is that it can produce the eye-consciousness having the aspect of a flower.

The Great Exposition, one of the Buddhist schools, does not accept the theory of aspect. They say that eye-consciousness has direct contact with the object itself. This is very difficult to accept. The viewpoint of the other schools, such as the Followers of Scripture, is that things do have aspects through which the consciousness perceives the object.

The theory founded by modern scientists which accepts the aspect of the object through which it is perceived by the consciousness seems to share this more logical background.

This eye-consciousness perceives a form and not a sound; that is the imprint of the sense-organ on which it depends.

Such an eye-consciousness is also the product of the preceding moment of the consciousness which gives rise to it.

Although we talk about states where gross levels of mind are dissolved, the subtle consciousness always retains its continuity. If one of the conditions, such as the preceding moment of consciousness, is not complete, then even when the sense organ and the object meet they will not be able to produce the eye-consciousness which sees.

Mental consciousnesses are very different, and the ways in which the sensory and mental consciousnesses perceive an object are also unique.

Because sensory consciousness is non-conceptual, it perceives all the qualities, all the attributes of the object collectively.

But when we talk in general about mental consciousness, it is mainly conceptual. It perceives an object through an image. It apprehends an object by excluding what it is not.

One has really to think deeply about the question of whether consciousnesses are created or produced from chemical particles of the brain mechanism. In recent years I have met scientists in the fields of nuclear physics as well as neurology and psychology. Very interesting. We have to learn certain things from their experiments, from their latest findings. They seem to show a keen interest to know more about Buddhist explanations of consciousness and mind.

I have raised this topic with many people but have never found a satisfactory answer: If we adhere to a position that consciousness is nothing other than a product of the interaction of particles within the brain, then we have to say that each consciousness is produced from particles in the brain.

In that case, take the possible consequences in relation to this rose. One person might have the view that this is a plastic rose; he has a mistaken consciousness. Later he might tend to doubt, thinking it might not be a plastic rose, so the mistaken consciousness now turns into a wavering doubt. And then he presumes that it is a natural flower; this is still only a presumption. Then finally, through some circumstances like touching it or smelling it, he finds that it is a natural rose.

During all these stages, he has a consciousness directed towards one single object, but he is passing through these different stages of consciousness: from the mistaken view, to doubt, to presumption, to valid cognition, to valid perception. It is clear that he is experiencing different kinds of consciousnesses. But how does one explain the changes in chemical particles during these stages?

To use another example: We see a person and think he is our friend. But that person is not our friend. We mistook him. Then again that consciousness is mistaken. When we saw that person we had an erroneous consciousness, but the moment someone told us that this was not our friend it caused a change from that mistaken perception of the person into a valid perception.

The question of the experiences of great meditators arises. When a practitioner enters into a very deep state of meditation, breathing and also the heartbeat stop. Some of my friends who practice these things remain without heartbeat and breathing for quite some time. If someone remains in such a state for a few hours, what is the function of the brain during that time?

On the basis of all this I am trying to argue that there exists a phenomenon called consciousness, which has its own entity apart from the brain cells. The gross level of consciousness is very closely related to the physical body, but is also naturally related to the brain.

Consciousness of its own nature is something distinct. The subtler consciousness becomes more independent of the physical particles.

That is why the physical functions of a meditator stop when he reaches a very deep state of consciousness, yet consciousness remains. At that moment, because the physical functions have stopped, the gross level of consciousness is no more, but the subtle level of consciousness becomes more intensely manifest.

There are different types of consciousness: those during the waking state; during the dream state; during very deep sleep; and then during the state of unconsciousness, e.g. in a faint.

According to highest yoga tantra, the actual process of death is preceded by eight dissolution processes. There are the dissolutions of the elements of earth, water, fire, wind and space. And then we go through processes known as white appearance, red increase, black near-attainment, and the clear light of death.

Some people experience these dissolutions up to a certain stage (of death) and then turn back. I have met some people who experienced this and were fascinated by these unusual events. They came and asked me for an explanation. I think that according to the highest Buddhist tantras they seem to have experienced a certain deep level of consciousness and then returned.

After the experience of the clear light of death, when the being is in the process of taking birth into a realm where there is an intermediate state or *bardo*, then he goes through this intermediate stage. When, for example, the being is taking rebirth as a human, he experiences the intermediate state before the consciousness enters the womb. Thus the life process begins and ends with the experience of the clear light.

If we do not accept continuity of consciousness, the question of the evolution of the world itself arises. If we accept the Big Bang theory, then what was the reason for the Big Bang to have happened?

If we adhere to a position saying that things can exist without any cause, then we will find a lot of logical inconsistencies. But if, on the other hand, we accept the theory of a creator, in that case too there arise a lot of logical inconsistencies.

According to the Buddhist point of view, there are sentient beings who take part in the environment or natural habitat, and the universe evolves. We accept beginningless continuity of consciousness. Although such a position poses fewer questions, some questions still arise. For instance, why is there no beginning and no end of subtle consciousness? In enlightenment, or Buddhahood subtle consciousness still exists without end.

The basic reason suggesting the existence of rebirth is that consciousness requires a substantial cause, an earlier moment of consciousness. If we look further for the continuity of consciousness of this life, like at the time of conception, then this continuity can be traced back to the previous life. By extension, there is no reason why the continuity of consciousness should cease at the last moment of this life, at the time of death.

For this reason we have to be concerned about our future lives. Whether we will have good or unfortunate future rebirths depends on our actions in this life. So while involving ourselves busily in the affairs of this life, we should not neglect to think about the future.

Ignorance: Grasping at an Independent Self

There may be many different causes for our suffering, but the prevailing one is attachment and desire. For this reason desire is very strongly stressed in the twelve links of interdependent origination, where it occupies two links: the eighth and the ninth.

Desire has its root in ignorance. There are many different types of ignorance, but the one we are talking about here is the ignorance which misconceives the nature of reality.

No matter how forceful our ignorant mind appears, it has no valid foundation.

The ignorance we are concerned with here has two parts: the self-grasping attitude focused on the person; and the self-grasping attitude focused on objects.

Within the context of suffering and pleasure, all phenomena are divided into two: the instrument or that which causes suffering; and the one who takes part in it, or suffers. Having divided phenomena into two, the being and external phenomena, then we explain the self-grasping attitude focused on the person as the ignorance which grasps at the supposed true existence of the being. The self-grasping attitude focused on objects is the ignorance which grasps at the supposed true existence of external phenomena.

Now here we can test ourselves. When we recollect happy memories or a very anxious time, when we go through fluctuating states of mind like thinking, "I had such great pleasure at that time," or "I had such a hard time," then we should ask ourselves, "What is that 'I', that self that I feel so vividly?"

Reflect whether you identify that 'I' with your body or with your consciousness.

According to the Buddhist point of view, when we recollect that extreme feeling in our life, when we have a very vivid impression, or feeling of that 'I' which went through those experiences, at that point the 'I' appears to us like the master and our aggregates such as body and mind like the servants. The 'I' seems to employ them.

But that impression is wrong. Such an independent 'I' which acts like a master does not exist.

Buddhists propound the theory of selflessness. This does not mean that Buddhists negate the existence of the conventional self or 'I'. There does exist a self which accumulates actions, which undergoes the consequences. But Buddhists negate the misconceived notion of an independent self.

In the same way, if we logically analyze the aggregates, which comprise form, feeling, cognition or perception, volition and consciousness, we do not find their essence. When we say "my body", that again is a kind of combination of head, arms, legs, and torso. All that we call body.

When we then analyze whether head, arms, legs, or torso are our body, we find they are not our body but that they are parts of an entity which is known as body.

In the same way, a hand is a collection of such things as these different fingers. But when we further analyze finger or hand we cannot find the essence in them.

The same is the case down to the smallest particles. When we reach subatomic levels where we cannot physically divide the particles, they still retain the identity of form and have directional parts.

In the same way let us talk about phenomena like consciousness, which do not have form. They do not have directional parts, but they have instances of moments. For example, when we say, 'my thought of today,' this is a whole concept labelled on the collection of the continuity of consciousness which we experience during the twenty-four hours of the day. We find that even the concept of the mind is posited or labelled on the collection of many different instances.

When we look at a thing like 'my own mind' superficially, it appears to our consciousness as a kind of solid or independently existing mind; just as when we reflect on the concept of 'I', a very self-sufficient independent 'I' like a master appears to us. In the same way, when we look at external phenomena, then it seems that they do have some kind of independent existence in their own right. But they do not.

Let us take the example of a government. We can say 'the government says,' 'the government thinks.' But then when we ask whether the government has a mouth or a tongue we get an uncomfortable feeling.

Let's consider another concept, that of a tailor. We see that it comes from a function, the action of tailoring. Without this action, how can the concept of tailor come about; and without tailor, how can we talk about sewing? We find that these two are interdependent.

All things are like this. When we analyze them, we cannot find anything. We just have to leave things as they are, accept them at their face value.

Take emptiness as an example. There is emptiness as a function, and therefore there must be some basis which allows this function.

Again if we investigate what emptiness is, we can vaguely say that it is the absence of independent existence. Then when we go into detail and when we follow the same process and search for the essence of 'this emptiness,' 'that emptiness,' even 'emptiness as ultimate reality,' we cannot find it.

We find that emptiness depends very much on the ways in which it is qualified, the object by which it is qualified. Therefore, what is the meaning of dependent arising? It finally will be traced to the point where we say that it is only the creation of the conceptual mind. How is it created by the conceptual mind? Again there follow a lot of questions.

Therefore Buddhists say that when we search analytically, there is no answer. This is not an indication that things do not exist, but it is an indication that the way in which things exist is relative. They exist in dependence on other factors.

When we experience a negative state of mind through hatred or desire, that is caused by our concept of something as good or bad. Then in turn we will find that our concept of good or bad is very much polluted by a special goodness or badness superimposed on the object, which in turn is caused by holding something as truly good or truly bad.

Buddhists say that all these negative states of mind have their root in the ignorance which grasps at the true existence of phenomena.

The wisdom which realizes that things do not exist inherently or independently on their own serves as the direct opponent factor for eliminating the misconceptions that we have of grasping at things as truly existent.

That is how we conclude that the self-grasping attitude is a state of mind which can be eliminated.

After we have meditated and reflected on the emptiness of true existence of oneself as person and of things we should go into a crowd of people and quietly watch them. We can still recognize the people for who they are, but the way we perceive them has subtly changed.

If through employing the correct opponent forces we can eliminate the ignorance of grasping at true existence of all things, then we shall achieve actual liberation, nirvana.

As we have the potential to achieve nirvana, to find release from this cycle of existence, we should develop the strong intention to take advantage of our situation.

Visualizing the Object of Refuge

The next part of the text explains the importance of not confining this intention to achieving enlightenment to ourselves alone but of extending it to all sentient beings.

With that motivation we engage in the practice of taking refuge. That is to say, we take refuge in the Buddha, Dharma and Sangha. For this, we visualize all sentient beings around us.

The visualization for this practice is as follows. In the space before us, about four feet in front of us at the level of our eyes, the objects of refuge should be visualized in the nature of light. If we visualize the deities as bright rays of light it will help to eliminate mental sinking, or sleepiness. On the other hand, if we visualize the deities as something heavy and solid, this will help us to reduce mental excitement, which otherwise might disturb us.

To the right of Buddha we visualize the Bodhisattva Avalokiteshvara, white in colour, which signifies purity.

Manjushri is to the Buddha's left and is yellow. Yellow signifies increase. Manjushri is the embodiment of increasing wisdom.

Meditating on Avalokiteshvara will increase the force of compassion and meditating on Manjushri will increase the force of wisdom.

Then we visualize Vajrapani in front of the Buddha. Vajrapani has slightly wrathful features. If you have indications of mysterious or invisible obstacles, then the recitation of the mantra of Vajrapani will help to overcome them.

Finally we visualize Arya Tara behind Buddha. The practice for longevity is mainly done on the basis of meditation on Tara.

One recommendation as to how to visualize all sentient beings is that on our right side we visualize all our male relatives starting from our father, and on our left side all our female relatives starting from our mother. Behind us are all the other sentient beings except our enemies; they are in front of us. We visualize all these different sentient beings in the aspect of human beings actively undergoing the sufferings of their different kinds of rebirths.

Reflect on the fact that just as we strongly desire happiness and want to avoid suffering, the other beings have the same natural tendencies to desire happiness and not suffering. Particularly if there are beings whom you regard as enemies or whom you suspect of wishing to harm you, or people who irritate you or give you a feeling of unease when you see them, deliberately visualize them in front of you and think, "Their nature as sentient beings is just like mine. He or she also wants happiness, not suffering."

In this respect we have the same nature, the same position. It is no use to feel angry or have bad feelings towards them. If we develop a negative attitude, negative feeling, it won't harm them. We only lose our own peace of mind. If our negative feelings hurt the others, then they might be worthwhile to have. But this is not the case.

For example if I, the Dalai Lama, as a Tibetan were to feel very negative towards the Chinese or towards Chen Ching, nothing would happen to them. They would remain relaxed, wouldn't they? But I would lose my own small peace of mind. Bad feelings towards others are actually self-destructive.

For that reason, the enemy is deliberately visualized in front.

Meditating in that way, recite these sacred words twenty-one times many times as you can: *Namo Buddhaya, Namo Dharmaya, Namo Sanghaya.*

If you have the wish and the time you can do the following practice. While you recite the refuge formula with a motivation of compassion and with conviction, you visualize that light-rays emanate from the objects of refuge and enter your body and those of the sentient beings around you.

Visualize that all negative attitudes like desire, ignorance, and anger within yourself and other sentient beings are pacified by these waves of light-rays.

Generating the Mind of Enlightenment

To generate the mind of enlightenment we reflect on the fact that, just like ourselves, all other sentient beings equally have the natural tendency to desire happiness and the wish to avoid suffering. The only difference is that I am a single person whereas the others are limitless in number. In other words one is in the minority; the others are the majority.

Again, reflect that just as I want happiness, so they too want happiness; I do not want suffering, and they do not want suffering; and that there is a clear relation between me and them. We depend on others; without others we cannot gain any happiness: not in the past, not today, and not in the future.

If we think more about others' benefit and welfare, ultimately it is we ourselves who will reap the benefit.

Thinking on these lines we find that when comparing the two, ourselves and others, the others are more important. We come to the conclusion that the fate of ourselves is a question of only one person. If it is the case that one has to undergo suffering in order to bring about happiness for the infinite number of others, then it is really worthwhile to suffer. On the other hand, if in order to achieve happiness for one then many others will have to suffer, then something is wrong in the perspective.

To approach the practice of cultivating the mind of enlightenment, the aspiration to achieve enlightenment for the sake of all sentient beings, first we have to achieve equanimity. Equanimity in this context means to cultivate an equal state of mind towards all sentient beings, one that is not affected by desire for friends, hatred for enemies, or indifference towards neutral people. We are seeking an equal state of mind towards all sentient beings.

Here it is useful to visualize three people in front of you: one neutral, one your closest friend, and one your worst enemy. Then let your feelings react. For each of the three people you will have a different feeling. Why?

This person has done me some good, so I regard him as my friend. But is there a guarantee he will always be a good friend? Even in this lifetime? Not so sure! Even in this lifetime there were close friendships that are now just so-so. These changes happen easily. That is reality.

Because of this, there is no reason to feel such deep attachment. Feeling close is good, but being blindly attached is not good. Then there is the side of the enemy. Today he acts as enemy, but again it is not certain for how long.

Thinking in this way will naturally equalize your feelings. Yes, this is a good friend, and this is a bad enemy, alright; but do not have an unbalanced mental attitude. That is the first step.

Secondly we have to contemplate the recognition that all sentient beings have been our own mothers in one lifetime or another.

Generally speaking, there are four types of birth: birth from the womb, from an egg, from heat, and miraculous birth.

In birth from the womb or from an egg, we need a mother. Today, for example, I could feel, though my mother of this lifetime passed away some years ago, that at one or another time all of you have been my mother. We may logically not be certain about it, but we can develop the feeling that you have been my mother.

On the basis of that, we should reflect on kindnesses received when these beings were my mother in past lives. In the same way, we then meditate on others as having been our own fathers or close relatives or friends of past lives.

If that is the case, then we should remember that their kindness towards us must have been boundless. Since the number of our lifetimes is beginningless, we must have been conceived limitless times, on many occasions a child to each of them.

That is the third stage.

The fourth is the special recollection of kindness. This really extends not only to our close relatives but to all sentient beings.

Our very survival depends entirely on others. For example, if our clothes are of cotton, cotton comes from the fields, from those labourers who worked on them not only in this generation but in previous generations. Then our houses, this room for example. Today it is rather hot, but otherwise we are very comfortable. This comfort is the result of hardships endured by many workers who gave their energy, who sweated and worked until they had sores on their hands and had bent backs.

Up to the present day our survival has depended on food. Thinking of myself, if I imagine all those loaves of bread I have consumed piled up; they would make quite a mountain. And the milk I have drunk would make a pond. If one is not vegetarian, then one consumes another mountain of meat. Vegetarians eat all sorts of fruits and vegetables. All this does not come from the sky. It does not appear from nowhere, but is produced through the hard work of many labourers.

And people's big names. Even fame comes from others. If there were only one single person, then there would be no possibility of becoming famous. Fame comes through many mouths. That also depends on others.

Food depends on others; clothing depends on others; housing depends on others.

We may think, "Oh, but I paid for all these things, I bought them for a certain amount of money. Without money I cannot get food or anything else."

But that money did not come from your own mouth either. It came through the hands of many people. The very existence of our lives depends entirely on others. Then you may feel, "Yes, these are facts, but the others did not deliberately help me. They did it as a by-product of their efforts to survive."

That is true. But I cherish many things that do not return my concern. For example, if my watch fell down on the floor and broke, I would feel some kind of a loss. This does not mean that this watch has some feeling for me or is kind to me. It is useful to me, so I care.

In the same way, all those people may not have done anything for us deliberately; but as their work is useful to us we should recognize and remember their kindness. We must be aware of the fact that although others do not have the motivation to help us, we depend on their contribution and efforts for our own survival.

Thinking on these lines and reflecting on the kindness of others becomes a very extensive practice.

The practice of compassion, kindness and altruism is something very excellent. Sometimes I am fascinated by the power of the human brain. Our human heart can produce such an altruistic state of mind, one that can hold others more dear than oneself. These things are really remarkable.

We cannot practice like this without other beings. One of the most important conditions is living beings. Without others we cannot practice compassion; without others we cannot practice love, genuine kindness, altruism, the mind of enlightenment.

There is no question about it. We do respect the Buddhas, Bodhisattvas and the higher beings, but in order to cultivate these good qualities, sentient beings are more important than Buddhas. On the ordinary level, our very survival depends on the kindness of other sentient beings, and even the realization of the path that one travels during spiritual purification depends on others.

For example, in order to practice genuine compassion or altruism, we need tolerance. Without tolerance, it is impossible to practice. Anger and hatred are the greatest obstacles to compassion and love. To minimize anger and hatred, tolerance is the key factor. In order to practice tolerance we need an enemy. The enemy will not want to help us deliberately, but because of our enemy's actions we get the opportunity to practice tolerance.

The golden opportunity is when we face an enemy. All sentient beings, but particularly our enemies, are very important for our mental development. Our spiritual practice depends entirely on others, and our very survival also depends on others. From that point of view, not only our close friends but all sentient beings are something very important to us.

That is the fourth step in the meditation.

The fifth step is about how to develop the thought of repaying the kindness of others.

The sixth step is equalizing oneself with others. The meaning of this is to realize that just as we ourselves do not desire suffering and wish for happiness, in the same way other sentient beings have the same natural tendencies. Thinking like this, we develop this equality of equalizing oneself with others.

We should think of others as part of our own body. In times of danger you need to protect all parts of your body.

Your attitude to other sentient beings should be that they are 'mine'. Then when something hurts another being it will hurt us.

When we expand that kind of feeling to all sentient beings, then they all become like members of our own family. If anyone gets hurt, we feel it as we feel our own pain. This is the sixth stage.

The seventh stage is to reflect on the many disadvantages of the self-cherishing thought. I often tell people that a very self-centered motivation, although it comes from the selfish wish for something good for oneself, in the end brings many problems. Killing, stealing, lying: all these actions are bad, not only from the religious point of view, but also according to the law. All these negative actions arise due to selfishness.

On a human level, fighting between husband and wife, parents and children, neighbour and neighbour, nation and nation, is due to internal confusion. All these negative, unfortunate actions are ultimately due to selfishness.

On the other hand, altruism is really the key source of happiness. If we help other people, if we show other people openness and sincerity, then we will greatly benefit ourselves as well. For example, we will easily make friends. I often feel that though we Tibetans are refugees, and are stateless people, as long as we are sincere and honest and also have a smile we will easily make friends. Even if we end up in the Soviet Union or wherever, we will find good friends. But if we are selfish and look down on other people, then we could not find friends anywhere.

Cultivating the thought of cherishing others more than ourselves produces great benefits. Our spiritual development, achievement of higher states, higher rebirth in future lives, and also the achievement of liberation and enlightenment all depend on cherishing others.

The result of stealing or killing sentient beings out of a selfish motivation is suffering and a short life. The result of protecting the lives of others out of an altruistic attitude is good rebirth and a long life.

The result of stealing is poverty; giving freely results in wealth. Telling lies results in confusion; and speaking the truth results in mental clarity.

Every self-centered action committed without regard for the welfare of others brings suffering; every selfless action brings gain.

Be it a question of different experiences on our own ordinary level or on the spiritual path, there is this fluctuation of positive and negative consequences which are products of either a selfish or an unselfish attitude.

The ninth stage is the actual thought of exchanging oneself with others. This is a state of mind which was initiated in an earlier process. Here we have the natural feeling to benefit other sentient beings.

Here we engage in the meditation of "giving and taking." We visualize taking on ourselves the difficulties of others, which is to emphasize our practice of compassion. Then we visualize giving other sentient beings both happiness and its causes. This strengthens our practice of love.

Next follows what is known as the special attitude, the thought of universal responsibility. This is facilitated as a result of the earlier meditations.

It is this thought that eventually gives rise to the mind of enlightenment, the aspiration to achieve highest enlightenment for the sake of all sentient beings. This is the eleventh and final step of the meditation.

In this system both the tradition for cultivating the mind of enlightenment as explained by Asanga and the tradition explained by Shantideva are integrated.

On the basis of the above motivation recite the following verse.

To the Buddha, the Dharma and the Supreme Community
I turn for refuge until enlightenment is gained.
By the strength of my practices, like the six perfections,
May enlightenment be attained for the benefit of all.

Repeat these words with a strong feeling of genuine altruism, the words acting like fuel so that the actual fire burns within yourself.

Repeat the passage three times or more. This can be done in English or your own mother-tongue.

Questions and Answers

Question: Your Holiness, I can understand that it helps people to accept the fluctuations in life better if it is said that they are due to past karma and that it helps to restrain actions in this life when we say that if we do something bad in this life it will affect our future lives.

But is it necessary that one must believe in future and past lives to live within the right lines?

His Holiness: Certainly not. I usually say that whether you are a believer or nonbeliever, you should be a kind-hearted person. That can be developed without acceptance of past or future lives, or without the acceptance of Buddhist or karmic theory. This is religion in itself.

I strongly feel that even anti-religious people, like Communists for example, can be very good-hearted. I have personally met several such people, who sacrificed their own lives for the benefit of the masses. They did this through their inborn qualities. People with good hearts do exist without believing in any Buddhist theory of rebirth.

I usually say that love and kindness are a universal religion. Today we are discussing Buddhism, and so I am talking about these things from the Buddhist point of view. If someone without these spiritual attitudes simply tries to be a good person, that is certainly possible, and he will succeed.

However, if a person does not accept the existence of a completely enlightened state, then the question of the mind of enlightenment cannot arise, because this is a state mind that aspires to the achievement of Buddhahood.

Question: Your Holiness, when you talk of subtle consciousness, is there a distinction between consciousness in itself, consciousness of something and consciousness for something?

His Holiness: Generally speaking, it is very difficult to imagine a consciousness without any object because the very term consciousness means to be conscious of something, an object.

I think the term consciousness is applied to the gross level of the mind from the point of view of action. The subtle consciousness becomes obvious in ordinary persons only in an unconscious state, for example in a faint.

When we consider the eight dissolution processes at death, the seventh is black near-attainment. This is divided into two: the first part is still retaining a subtle memory; in the second part we lose that also. We have this experience of clear light by the force of our own karmic actions.

This is like a natural process of dissolution where the aggregates, which we obtained as a consequence of our own karmic actions, cease. We go through that process naturally.

There is a possibility of experiencing such a state of clear light through training in yoga, utilizing the subtle energies and so forth. Here the meditator, by the force of his realizations, brings about this experience through meditation. He experiences the subtle level of consciousness and remains conscious of it. He does not lose control.

The meditator has to direct that type of experience to reality, the nature of emptiness.

Question: If death is the ultimate state of consciousness, then what about ghosts? Have you ever come across any?

His Holiness: I do remember that as a child I was very much afraid of ghosts.

In Buddhism we have six types of rebirths. This division is made on the basis of the degree of suffering or pleasure. When the division is made on the basis of having gross or subtle levels of form or feeling or mind, then we divide sentient beings into three realms: the desire realm, form realm and formless realm.

Ghosts can belong to any of these three realms or states. Just like human beings, some are positive, some are negative, some are cruel, and some are kind. Just like that.

Question: Your Holiness, is it possible to grasp dependent arising without the accumulation of merit and without the purification of delusions?

His Holiness: One can realize dependent arising while still having delusions, on the basis of this ordinary mind. Investigate emptiness on the basis of this relativity theory, and then you can realize, can understand emptiness; intellectually thinking about it, meditating on it, you can feel it.

Here we have to distinguish between the consciousness which realizes the nature of dependent arising, and the inferential understanding of emptiness.

In order to have direct experience, that is, the realization of emptiness or dependent arising, one has to decrease the force of delusions which we ordinary beings have. Then meditating on emptiness directly will serve as further purification.

You will find that realization of emptiness is not so difficult.

Question: Your Holiness, you mentioned that the 'I' is like a master. I could not fully understand what you meant. Is there something in us which makes us think or act, the ego?

His Holiness: We cannot deny the existence of an 'I'. We cannot find it, but it does exist. It exists as a result of imputation. The self or 'I' is not self-sufficient, but many of the ancient, non-Buddhist schools explain it as a self-sufficient entity separate from the aggregates. They say that while the body changes, the 'I' is permanent, a sort of one-ness. Such an 'I' Buddhists do not accept. Such an 'I' we call *atma* and the very word *atma* symbolizes something solid or independent.

Obviously when our mind changes then the 'I' changes automatically.

When we have some pain we can say 'I am sick,' 'I have a pain.' This is not the 'I', but through it we can express ourselves.

Question: Your Holiness, you told us there is no beginning and no end. We are also told that the middle, the so-called phenomenal universe, does not exist; it too is illusion. No beginning, no middle, no end. Where do we stand?

His Holiness: Buddha himself has said in the lines which I mentioned earlier, "Something which is produced from a cause or condition is not produced."

This means that they are produced and they are not produced at the same time. Buddhists accept the beginninglessness and endlessness of consciousness because different functions and levels in consciousness are perceived.

Having accepted such a position, one can logically explain and become convinced of the different functions that are possible on the basis of such a premise.

Since different kinds of function are possible, we will find that there is no truly existing thing, self-existing thing, which cannot be affected by these different functions, and that therefore their nature is empty.

Since on the basis of this emptiness all these different types of seemingly contradictory functions are possible, they are like illusions.

Emptiness in the sense of *shunyata* is explained on the basis of something that exists, which has connections with reality. Any phenomenon has emptiness as its own nature, which is the absence of its true existence.

Emptiness is a quality, the ultimate quality of things. For example, the phenomena which depend on causes have the quality of momentary change. Furthermore, how does momentary change become possible? Through emptiness, through its own quality.

When we say quality, there must be some basis for it. Without that basis, there can be no quality.

6

The Buddha's Way

Buddha and two disciples, Shariputra and Maudgalyayana

Meditation on the Mind of Enlightenment

The Indian Master Haribhadra said in his writings that the mind of enlightenment is a state of consciousness which is induced by the wish for all sentient beings to be free from suffering and is complemented simultaneously by the intention to achieve enlightenment for the sake of others.

When we talk about the aspiration to achieve enlightenment, it is said that this aspiration is characterized by the compassion which is directed towards sentient beings, and is a wisdom which is directed towards enlightenment.

In order to achieve enlightenment, first of all it is necessary to achieve nirvana. Perception of nirvana itself depends on the realization of emptiness.

In the basic practice of taking refuge, which is the action that determines whether one is a Buddhist or not, it seems that for the refuge to be ultimately effective one should have the realization of emptiness. Thus there exist many different levels in the practice of refuge.

Speaking about the procedure of the path, someone who is not a Buddhist can first try to cultivate an understanding of emptiness and through that realization can appreciate nirvana, the cessation of suffering.

This provides the basis for confidence in the Dharma. Then through this understanding, one can develop respect for the Buddha who taught it, and for the spiritual community who are in the process of the path.

Generally we divide practitioners into two types: those of high mental intensity, who follow the path mainly through reasoning; and those of ordinary caliber, who mainly rely on their faith.

The mode of procedure for the practitioner of high caliber is the one explained earlier, following the path mainly through reasoning.

When we have taken refuge in the Three Jewels, this indicates that we have become Buddhists.

However, whether or not we are Mahayana Buddhists is determined by whether or not we take our refuge on the basis of the altruistic aspiration to highest enlightenment. For this reason the process of taking refuge is conjoined to the thought of generating the aspiration to enlightenment.

The next stage in the meditation (*A Tantric Meditation*; See *Appendix*) involves the practice of accumulating merit by reciting the seven-limbed prayer.

The practice of the seven-limbed prayer has its source in the *Avatamsaka Sutra*. We can also find references to it in the *Prajnaparamita Sutra*.

The first of the seven limbs is that of offering prostrations. Since the words of the text are clear here, I do not think there is any need for further explanation. The practice of prostrations is to overcome conceit, pride.

The second limb is the practice of offering. This is an antidote to selfishness.

The third limb, the practice of purification, which is the acknowledgment of one's shortcomings and failings, is an antidote to all three mental poisons of desire, hatred and ignorance.

The practice of rejoicing, the fourth limb, is the antidote to jealousy.

The fifth limb, the practice of requesting the Buddhas to turn the wheel of Dharma, is the antidote to negative karma that one accumulated with regard to scriptures and other sacred objects.

The practice of requesting the Buddhas to remain without passing *Parinirvana* is the sixth limb. It is an antidote to negative karma accumulated by disparaging high beings.

The seventh limb, the practice of dedication, is the antidote to wrong views, chiefly the wrong views which deny the law of causality, the law of karma, thinking that effects are not produced from their causes.

Concentration Meditation

If anyone wants to practice deep concentration or calm abiding (*shamatha*) meditation, then as we already discussed we need a completely isolated place to spend a few months. I expect that this is not practical for many of you. But in your daily life some kind of practice of calm abiding is still possible. For this practice we can take any object as the focus of our concentration.

We will take as our object the visualization we are using in our meditational text (*Appendix*), that is, the gathering of Buddha and the four Bodhisattvas: Avalokiteshvara, Manjushri, Vajrapani and Tara.

At this point, to practise calm abiding meditation, we relax our awareness of the four Bodhisattvas in the visualization, and concentrate on Buddha, the central figure.

As I mentioned earlier, visualize that the Buddha radiates with brilliant lights, yet his body is something extremely dense. This helps to stabilize the mind and to eliminate darkness.

To gain clarity of visualization, it is helpful to first closely study a large, detailed statue of the Buddha and then try to imagine it during meditation.

Having conjured up this imagine in your meditation, then you should try to retain it by the force of your mindfulness. You should apply your mental comprehension to the object.

In order to achieve a perfect single-pointedness of the mind it is necessary to have two factors: stability of mind and clarity. In the writings of Maitreya and Asanga, five main obstacles to the achievement of single-pointed concentration and eight opponent forces are mentioned.

The first of the five obstacles is laziness. The antidote to laziness is the understanding of the great benefits of concentration and the strong aspiration to achieve such concentration. As an opponent force to laziness, we need confidence in the concentration method.

Quite apart from the meditator, even in day-to-day life some kind of acquaintance with calm abiding will give you sharpness of mind and help to reduce dullness, the feeling of tiredness. It contributes to the alertness of the mind. That is very useful.

It is impossible for a practitioner to achieve special insight *vipashyana*) without calm abiding.

There is no value in visualizing deities if you do not do so with a basic degree of meditative concentration. If we have strong concentration, then visualizing deities works. It has an effect. These things depend entirely on one's own quality of concentration.

The second factor that we require is the aspiration to achieve concentration, energy, and the physical and mental pliancies that are the result of concentration. These four are antidotes to laziness.

The second obstacle is forgetting the object of meditation. The antidote to this is mindfulness that retains the object.

The third obstacle is comprised of mental excitement and mental dullness. Their antidote is mental alertness.

As for these two obstacles, mental excitement and mental dullness, they can be described as having various levels of subtlety. Some are gross, and others are quite subtle.

There is a particular state of mind called mental torpor. This is the cause of mental dullness. This type of mind is such that even in our meditation there is a total blank, no clarity, no image of the object nor any alertness from the side of the subject.

Now let us talk about that mental dullness where there is no clarity of the object. It can also be translated as mental sinking, when our mental force is in a sinking state.

Gross mental sinking is when we lose the object of meditation, and subtle mental sinking is when we do not retain the object clearly.

Mental excitement is a state of mind where our concentration is lost and our mind is scattered over all kinds of objects.

A subtle form of this mental excitement is when we still focus on the object, but the major part of the concentration is diverted. To protect ourselves from these obstacles, we have to use the antidote mental alertness. The cause of mental sinking is a mind that is too relaxed.

The cause of mental excitement is a concentration that is too tense, almost strained. So as not to encounter any of these obstacles, one has to find a balanced state of mind through one's own experience.

What are the ways to overcome mental sinking and mental dullness?

We have to tighten or relax the intensity of our concentration and alertness, depending on which of the two is appropriate to the situation.

The very subtle form of mental sinking can be overcome by increasing the intensity of our concentration. If we experience gross mental sinking, then it is better to interrupt the meditation for a while and instead recollect a pleasant experience that can induce a feeling of happiness. This will help to stimulate the mind. Or we can go outside for a relaxed stroll.

In case of subtle mental excitement, simply reduce the intensity of concentration. Alternatively when confronted by gross mental excitement, then it is advisable to recollect something sad, to calm the sense of excitement. In any case, to overcome both obstacles we will have to work on ourselves and find a balanced state of concentration through our own experience.

There are various approaches to the practice. These include concentration without an external object, concentration on certain mantras, syllables, or on light at certain important energy-centers. This is explained in highest yoga tantra. That is concentration on an internal object.

There is concentration on mind itself. At the beginning, this is something quite difficult because the object on which one tries to focus is mind, and the agent itself which we employ is mind. At the initial stage, it is a practice where you develop the intention to focus your concentration on the mind, and then you retain that very intention by the force of your mindfulness.

Until you have acquainted yourself through long practice, it is very difficult to concentrate on the mind. We always talk about mind, and we use it, but it is very difficult to perceive the mind.

The first of the next two obstacles is not to apply the proper antidotes when we experience the obstacles of excitement or mental sinking. The second is over-application of the antidotes.

There are nine stages for the cultivation of mental concentration, and when we reach the seventh or eighth stage, the force of vulnerability to obstacles is almost overcome. If we still applied the antidotes, it would harm instead of benefit us. At that point we have to apply equanimity as an antidote.

There are different types of equanimity. One instance is a neutral feeling. Then there is the equanimity of non-application of antidotes when they are not necessary. Another type is where we cultivate equanimity focussed on all sentient beings, i.e., being neutral toward all sentient beings.

These are the five obstacles and the eight antidotes to overcome them. When we are engaged in such intense practices, it is important to observe one's diet. To be a vegetarian is very beneficial.

From the point of view of Tibetan medicine, if one has been a vegetarian from the beginning, then that is safest but if one becomes a vegetarian at a later stage of life, then there is the danger of developing energy disorders. As a result, one experiences a hissing sound in one's ears or sweating in the palms, or one becomes prone to agitation. These are great hindrances to concentration. Otherwise, to be a vegetarian is excellent.

Then I think, another factor is to eat less food at night. Fasting at night is best, or if not, take just a small meal.

Nor is it good to go to bed late. Go to bed early, and get up early. The best time for this type of meditation is at dawn.

Sometimes it may be useful to do the practice when you are already awake but the sensory consciousnesses are not yet active, a kind of half-sleep. If you can develop a way to practise at that time, you might find it easier to realize some kind of clear light. That depends on the qualification of the individual.

There are various other methods explained in detail in highest yoga tantra. However, without initiation it is not permissible to practise them.

One interesting technique is that of the dream state yogas. To practise them we should realize that we are dreaming, and then engage a certain practice deliberately. Because our mind has become already more subtle, then with little effort a still deeper state of consciousness can be utilized.

When we can do that we can develop a dream body. This special dream body is something separate from our physical body. It is a subtle body, and it can go to many places and do many things. I think this body is the best secret agent. Equipped with this technique, one can fulfill one's responsibilities. There is no danger of getting caught. Nobody else can see one's dream body.

This type of practice deals mainly with gaining control over the subtle body and subtle mind. That comes in tantric practice. There are cases where practitioners, because of old age or physical handicaps, are not able to see with their eyes, which are part of their gross body. But with this realization they are able to read the scriptures with the tips of their fingers. This is a power born from concentration, which is common to both Buddhist and non-Buddhist practitioners.

Mantra Recitation

After that we do the mantra recitation. Usually we have sadhanas or texts of meditation, and when we have done the meditation and still have time, then we recite mantras.

The seed-syllables of the deities are visualized according to the text. (See *Appendix*) These are: *Mum* (gold), *Hrih* (white), *Dhih* (yellow), *Hum* (blue), and *Tam* (green). We can visualize the mantras in any letters, such as Sanskrit, Roman or others.

Mu is the first syllable of Muni, the name of Buddha Shakyamuni. This *Mu* with a dot on top reads *Mum*. We can say that the dot, the bindu, the "emme" sound, symbolizes emptiness and *Mum* conventional reality. It shows the union of emptiness and the subject, conventional entity.

Hrih is the seed-syllable of Avalokiteshvara because *Hrih* is the seed-syllable of Amitabha, the Tathagata Family to which Avalokiteshvara belongs.

Dhih is the Sanskrit sound for wisdom. Manjushri is the deity of wisdom and knowledge, and this is his seed-syllable.

Hum is the seed-syllable of Vajrapani, who is the embodiment of Buddha's mind. *Hum* is also the seed-syllable of Akshobhya, the Tathagata Family to whom Vajrapani belongs.

Tam is the seed-syllable of Tara. In the same way as *Mu* is the first syllable of the name of Buddha, so *Ta* is the first syllable of Tara. The bindu on top of the syllable makes it *Tam*.

The colours of these letters correspond to the colours of their deities. Each of these syllables is surrounded by its mantra, and we should repeat all of them as many times as we can.

Om muni muni maha muniye svaha–this is the mantra of Buddha Shakyamuni. *Muni* means the Able One and *Maha muni* the Great Able One. According to etymological explanation, *Om* is a contraction of the three Sanskrit letters *AUM*. It symbolizes the body, speech and mind of the Buddhas, as well as the practitioner's body, speech and mind.

Om mani padme hum is the mantra of Avalokiteshvara.

Mani is the Sanskrit word for jewel, which symbolizes method. Method according to Tantrayana deity yoga in the Mahayana teachings means the mind of enlightenment, great compassion (*mahakaruna*), great loving kindness (*mahamaitri*).

Padme means lotus, and here it symbolizes wisdom, the wisdom which understands emptiness.

Hum symbolizes indivisibility.

Just as *Om* symbolizes both the body, speech and mind of the practitioner which are not purified and also the purified body, speech and mind of the Buddhas, similarly this *Hum* signifies that through our practice we can transform our impure body, speech and mind into the purified body, speech and mind of the resultant state. These three impure elements transform into three pure elements.

What is the method? This is symbolized in *Mani* and *Padme*, these two words which represent method and wisdom.

As I mentioned earlier, these are the mind of enlightenment, great compassion, also deity yoga, and the wisdom which understands emptiness, indivisibly united as symbolized by *Hum*.

These two method conjoined to wisdom, can transform impure body, speech and mind into purified ones.

This is the meaning of *Om mani padme hum*. Quite a famous mantra, isn't it? Many people know *Om mani padme hum*.

The literal meaning of this mantra is "Oh he holding a lotus and a jewel in his hands."

Om wagi shvari mum is the mantra of Manjushri. *Wagi* is Sanskrit for speech, and Ishvari is someone who is a master of it." He who is proficient in speech" is the meaning of this mantra.

Om vajra pani hum is the mantra of Vajrapani. *Pani* means hand. The Tibetan translation of Vajrapani is "Holding a vajra in the hand." The literal meaning of this mantra is "someone who is holding a vajra in his hand." In the definitive meaning of this mantra 'vajra' symbolizes the union of method and wisdom. If we have a vajra and bell, then vajra symbolizes method and bell symbolizes wisdom. If a vajra is by itself, then it symbolizes the union of method and wisdom.

Om tara tuttare ture svaha is the mantra of Tara. The Tibetan translation is Dolma, the one who liberates. *Tutta-re* signifies an even greater intensity of liberation. The Tibetan interpretation of *Svaha* is to stabilize, to lay a foundation.

The roots of the word "mantra" are *mana*, which means mind, and *tra*, which means protection. Thus the implication is the protection of the mind.

Mantra in the tantric context means protecting one's mind from ordinary appearance and ordinary grasping.

In deity yoga we try to develop the feeling of ourselves as a deity. When we meditate and concentrate on a deity, our eyes and ears can perceive ordinary things, but on the level of mental consciousness we have withdrawn all natural perception and appearance of ordinariness and remain in a divine state.

In that practice we are protected from ordinary feeling and appearance. This is the meaning of the word 'mantra.'

In Buddhism we have different types of mantras, such as mundane mantras, supramundane mantras, root mantras, essence or heart mantras, and near-essence mantras. These are four different types of mantra. Some have *Om* at the beginning but no *Svaha* at the end. Others have *Svaha* at the end. Then some have both, and some neither. We mainly recite Buddha's mantra *Om muni muni maha muniye svaha*.

When we look on Buddha as a teacher, then the four deities surrounding him are special manifestations of Buddha for special purposes. For example, when someone concentrates on developing a good heart, then he concentrates on the mantra of Avalokiteshvara, *Om mani padme hum*.

We also recite this mantra as a dedication when someone has passed away. When my mother passed away my brother and many people, including myself, recited *Om mani padme hum* a hundred thousand times and more. This is good for spiritual development with regard to method. This is what we usually do.

Om wagi shvari mum, the mantra of Manjushri, is very good for students. It helps to increase one's intelligence, one's sharpness of mind. Sometimes we recite *dhih dhih dhih dhih* a hundred and eight times or more without a break, no breathing in between. We take a deep inhalation at the beginning and then start *dhih dhih dhih....* This helps us to increase the power of memory.

Om vajra pani hum, the mantra of Vajrapani, helps to overcome invisible hindrances. Of course it is not good to be superstitious, but if without apparent reasons disturbing things happen continuously, then there might be some invisible obstacles at work. The recitation of this mantra will help to disperse them.

Om tara tuttare ture svaha, the mantra of Tara, is recited for longevity and when one is suffering from illness and is under medical treatment. It also helps when we are doing business.

The basic aim of reciting mantras is enlightenment for the sake of other beings, and while we are trying to achieve that through recitation of mantras, some temporary aims like long life, success or the increase of wisdom are also achieved.

Mantric techniques are also used for the fulfillment of various activities like pacification, increase, power or wrath. In order to harness the energy of mantras one has first to realize emptiness and *bodhichitta*, the aspiration to achieve highest enlightenment.

Meditation on Emptiness

To realize that all deceptive phenomena are the same in their nature of emptiness, we concentrate on emptiness. When meditation on the mind of enlightenment and also training in concentration have matured, then the practice of emptiness begins.

Generally it is not necessary to withdraw the appearance of the object when we meditate on emptiness, but as we are concerned herewith tantric practices, it is recommended that the appearance of the object is withdrawn.

We can start this practice in either of two ways: we can first dissolve all appearances and then meditate on emptiness; or first meditate on emptiness and then dissolve all appearance of the objects.

Now to explain briefly the actual meditation on emptiness. Here it is very important to identify what is to be negated.

The major Buddhist schools accept what are known as the four Buddhist seals. These four are as follows:

All products are impermanent;
All contaminated phenomena are in the nature of suffering;
All phenomena are selfless and empty; and
Nirvana alone is peace.

Here selflessness refers to the emptiness of a self-sufficient person.

Selflessness of phenomena is explained only by the Mahayana schools: the Mind-Only and the Middle Way.

The Mind-Only School, by relying on the *Sutra Unravelling the Thought of Buddha*, propounds the existence of two types of phenomena. One is that although form, for example, is the referent object of conceptual thought, it is not the referent object of the consciousness realizing it as from its own side. It is only a label, a referent of the term form and also the conceptual thought which gives the label. Therefore the absence of form as the referent of the term is one type of emptiness.

The other type of emptiness is the negation of existence of external objects as existing apart from mental projections. The Mind-Only School says that external things do not exist, that they are only mental projections. The presentation of emptiness of the Middle Way School is different. Although followers of the Mind-Only School refute true existence of external objects, they believe in the true existence of the subjective mind.

Looking from the point of view of the Middle Way School, we find that the followers of Mind-Only have fallen into the extremes both of eternalism or absolutism and of nihilism. Because they do not accept external objects they have fallen into the extreme of nihilism; and since they accept a truly existent subjective mind, they have fallen into the extreme of absolutism.

According to the Middle Way School, both external phenomena and the subjective mind do not exist truly, but both exist conventionally.

Within the Middle Way School, there are two divisions. One part of the school says that although external phenomena are not truly existent in the sense that they are not the objects of consciousness which analyzes its true nature, there is something on the part of the object, some kind of essence within the object itself, that we can find on analysis and which justifies its having such conventionalities. For example, when they search for the person or the self, they will finally come up with the statement "consciousness is the identity of the person," or things like that. They say that something exists from the side of the object.

Then there is the other part of the school which says that phenomena do not exist truly in the sense that they are not the object of their consciousness which sees its reality; and at the same time, even when we analytically search for the essence or the convention of something, we cannot find what it is. That is the other part of the school. The view of the latter is the more profound one for the reason that it has fewer inconsistencies.

When we examine the theories of the other schools, we will find many logical contradictions within their systems.

When the Middle Way thinkers propound the theory of emptiness, they do so by employing different kinds of reasoning. One of them is the analysis of the cause of phenomena, known as "the diamond silver of reasoning." This reasoning analyzes from the side of the effect of the thing.

Then there are reasonings where we search for four possibilities, analyzing both from the point of view of cause and from the point of view of the effect.

Another reasoning is known as the king of reasonings, the reason of dependent arising.

Still a different reasoning is that which observes the absence of singularity and plurality by analyzing the thing itself. Within the reasoning known as absence of singularity and plurality, there exist also different styles of observation.

Now I shall explain very briefly the meditation on emptiness within the reasoning of absence of singularity and plurality.

Firstly, in order to meditate on emptiness we have to identify the emptiness on which we are meditating, the thing to be negated. Unless we identify the object of negation, we cannot have the image of its absence.

For this it is more convenient first to reflect on one's own self.

When you have this natural feeling of "I go, I eat, I stay," just contemplate what kind of self or 'I' appears to your mind. Then try different techniques. As I mentioned earlier try to recollect unpleasant situations where, for example, you were unjustly blamed for something; or pleasant situations where you were praised. During such experiences you had a very fluctuating state of mind, and at that time it seemed you could sense that 'I', that self, quite clearly.

When this 'I' appeared to your mind, did it appear as something separate from your body and mind, like an independent entity? That type of 'I' or self, which appears to you so vividly that you feel you could put your finger on it, something independent from your own body and mind, that type of 'I' is the most misconceived projection, and that is the object of negation.

This is the first essential point, identifying what is to be negated.

The second essential point is to reflect whether, if such an 'I' or independent self exists, it does so as one with the body and mind; or truly separate from them; or if there is a third way in which it can exist.

You have to look at the different possibilities, and then you will find that, if it truly exists as an independent entity, it should be either one with the body and mind, the aggregates, or it should be separate, because there is no third-way of existence.

That is the second essential point.

The choices are that it is either one with the aggregates or totally different from them. Now reflect that, if it is one with the aggregates, then just as the self is one, body and mind should be one, because they are identified with the self. If the self is separate, then just as the aggregates are manifold, in the same way the self should be manifold.

Then contemplate that if this independent self or 'I' existed as something distinctly separate, truly apart from the aggregates, then it should be findable even after the aggregates ceased to exist. But this is not the case.

When you search by this mode of inquiry you will find that such an 'I' cannot be identified from the side of the aggregates.

Reasoning thus you will find that the independent 'I' or self that previously appeared to your consciousness is a misconception or projection. It does not exist.

For example, at dawn or dusk, when there is not much light, someone might get frightened and might mistake a coiled rope for a snake. Apart from the image of the snake in the mind of that person, there is no sense of true existence of snake on the part of the object, the rope.

It is the same with the aggregates. When you perceive the appearance of self in them, although such appearance seems to arise from within the aggregates, there is not the slightest particle which can be identified as the self within the aggregates. Just as in the earlier example wherein the snake is only a misconceived projection, there is no true existence of the snake.

In the same way, when we have the appearance or apprehension of person as distinct from the aggregates, from the side of the aggregates there is no true existence of the person; there is only a label imputed on the aggregates. As long as there is no essence existing on the part of the object concerned, in both cases they are the same.

As far as the status of the object from the side of the object is concerned, there is no difference at all between them. The difference has to come from the perceiving mind, from the side of the subject. When we label that coiled rope as a snake, that is a mistaken convention. After awhile the sun rises, we get a clear view of the object, and can dispel the misconception of that rope as a snake by valid cognition, a different type of consciousness.

That label of snake on the coiled rope can be harmful. However, in the case of a person although there is no objective reality, if you label the aggregates as the person, it serves the purpose of the convention. There is no other type of consciousness which can dispel that.

However, if we were to say that therefore there is no person at all, then our own experiences would contradict our false conclusion.

Hence the existence of the person has to be justified only from the subjective consciousness which gives the label. For this reason things are said to exist only nominally; there is no objective reality.

Questions and Answers

Question: In the type of special insight that focuses upon breathing, a dissolution of the body takes place because of the changing nature of the body, and you achieve a certain stage where you realize that everything is in a state of flux. How does that fit in with the doctrine of special insight meditation as taught in the Tibetan tradition?

His Holiness: There are two major types of special insight meditation. One of these focuses on conventional phenomena and the other on emptiness.

In special insight focused on conventional phenomena, there is one type where we concentrate on the breathing process. We can also do special insight practice in which we visualize deities, Buddha forms, emanating from ourselves and then absorbing back into us.

There is also a worldly special insight practice, where we focus on the faults of the desire realm and the advantages of the form and formless realms, the higher realms. This is a comparative special insight method.

These kinds of special insight meditation can be applied at the beginning, when we cultivate the motivation for the practice.

For example, when we meditate on the suffering nature of samsara, then we have to practice mindfulness of the body. Here in this practice we concentrate on the uncleanliness, impurity, and transitory nature of the body.

After that we practise mindfulness of feeling, mindfulness of the mind, and eventually mindfulness of phenomena.

During all these different practices of the four mindfulnesses, one can focus one's concentration on the breathing meditation process. The practice of breathing can be incorporated into any appropriate part of any practice.

The meaning of special insight meditation according to the Indian master Asanga is explained as being a state where we achieve mental subtleness after having employed observation.

While retaining the stability of concentration we apply reasoning. We achieve mental subtleness. The mind becomes more pliant. That state of mind is known as special insight.

Meditative calm, or mental tranquility, is a state of mind that is achieved through employing mostly absorbed, fixed meditation.

Generally when people talk about special insight I think they have this reasoning process in mind.

Question: Your Holiness, you were talking earlier about mantras and the effect that they can have. Some of them help to deepen our thinking. Others seem to help our concentration. But I wonder how a series of sounds can actually do that?

His Holiness: The oral repetition of the mantra is the literal mantra. While we are repeating the mantra we should also be reflecting on it's meaning, which is deeper than the mere sound.

How that type of recitation brings about those effects is difficult to explain. I think that when we recite mantras properly we increase the strength of our positive energy, our merit.

Another thing, of course, is some kind of blessing. The mantra was taught by certain forces, and through the passage of time many people have practised the same mantra.

I think that in this way the mantras themselves become blessed. As we discussed earlier, holy places can become blessed by holy people, and later these places are able to pass the blessings on to pilgrims or practitioners. The same is possible with mantras.

If one is engaged in the practice of the subtle energy yogas and in visualizing the energy channels, then there is a close link between mantra and the energy yogas that can be applied. But here we are not concerned with such practices, so I won't go into them. But in fact the main effect of the recitation of mantras comes in the practice of highest yoga tantra, where one engages in the methods that work with the subtle energies, drops and channels.

Question: Could you say something about nirvana?

His Holiness: First let me achieve it. (His Holiness pretends to sit in intense meditation. This is greeted by uproarious laugher).

The thing is that after we achieve final realization our entire attitude toward phenomena changes completely.

At present our minds are dominated by attachment, aversion, fear, and the host of negative thoughts and emotions.

Due to our negative thoughts, we cannot see or realize actual reality. There is some kind of colouring of our perception, and thus we do not see things simply as they are.

Due to the ignorance of grasping at true existence, everything appears as if it existed from its own side. A very strong, solid appearance is there with the object of perception, projected onto it.

When we reach nirvana, these negative or distorted states of mind are completely purified. As a result, one's whole attitude toward phenomena is different.

Question: But do you still respond to phenomena?

His Holiness: There is still the distinction between bad and good, negative and positive. Accordingly we can feel this is something good, that something bad.

There are various states of enlightenment, different "enlightenments." The highest of them all is Buddhahood, where even appearances of true existence are prevented.

We can feel there is a possibility to achieve such things. For example, we can see how our mind has changed since childhood, through its growth in knowledge and understanding. As a consequence our attitudes have changed. Similarly, if we meditate on emptiness consistently over a period of years we will be able to witness the same growth of our spiritual vision as we have witnessed in our worldly growth from child to adult. More time, more effort and, no doubt, more experience will follow.

At one time, I think in the late sixties or early seventies, I meditated quite intensely on emptiness.

One day I chanced upon a teaching by Je Tzongkhapa where he said, "The collection of the aggregates is not the self, nor is the self the continuity of the collection of the aggregates." When I read that statement, I became quite frightened.

Actually this was an explanation of the essence of one of the teachings of the Indian Master Nagarjuna,

A person is not the earth element,
Nor the water element, nor the fire element,
Nor the wind element.
At the same time there is no person who is
Apart from them.

The text also says that if you analytically search for the essence of a thing, this essence is not findable.

As a result of that moment of inspiration I gained some small realization, and over the next few days I noticed a transformation, a different feeling or attitude toward phenomena.

Question: Can one have an internal spiritual experience without having engaged in the formal trainings? I am thinking of the little known case of Younghusband, who apparently had a deep spiritual experience in Lhasa. At the time he was only about forty years old, and was one of the most promising young officers in the British Army. He resigned the military, set up his organization called Society for Spiritual Enlightenment, and devoted the rest of his life to this cause.

Is it not possible sometimes for some internal motivation or shock to one's system to produce a sudden preparation for intensive meditation, without going through these preliminary meditations?

His Holiness: That is possible. But according to the Buddhist explanation that possibility is not the consequence of effort or ability, not due to immediate circumstances, but behind that there are some other things. Full preparation is there, but it has waited for an opportunity. When that opportunity comes, the preparation bears fruit.

Question: Your Holiness, what exactly is tantra? And was it there from the time of Buddha, or did it come later?

His Holiness: There is a system of belief according to which the entire Mahayana doctrine is not considered to be a direct teaching of the Buddha. There is also a general view that tantra is much later.

On the other hand, if one does not accept Mahayana as an authentic teaching of the Buddha, then even Buddhahood itself is questionable. Therefore one would more or less have to conclude that the Mahayana is an authentic teaching of the Buddha.

The difference is that the Mahayana was taught by the Buddha to selective audiences and not at public events. For some time it remained a secret doctrine. Tantra is even more secret.

The turning of the open propagation of these different levels of doctrine also had something to do with the timing of the karmic maturation of the practitioners to be trained, that is, the spiritual development of the Buddhist civilizations.

It is not necessary to restrict the emergence of Mahayana and Tantrayana to the historical time of the Buddha Shakyamuni, however. In the Mahayana it is said that even though Buddha Shakyamuni passed away, nonetheless he is still regarded as being alive.

There are many stories of people receiving direct teachings from the Buddha. Historically Buddha never went to Tibet, but in reality there were many occasions when certain Tibetans with deep experience could see Buddha in their visionary states. They could directly receive teachings from the Buddha, while sitting there in a state of meditation.

In order to teach the various levels of doctrine the Buddha appeared in various forms to his disciples. In some cases he appeared as a monk, in other cases as Buddha Vajradhara. He also appeared as various mandala deities, and so forth.

Question: My query is about the Madhyamika system of Buddhist philosophy and their doctrine of emptiness. Is there a way of directly perceiving emptiness without practising special insight meditation?

His Holiness: In order to develop the wisdom that perceives emptiness it is not mandatory to develop special insight nor formal meditative absorption. That is a different question altogether. It is true that special insight meditation coupled with meditative absorption is very useful, but it is not the only way.

The actual experience of emptiness at the initial stage, the fresh realization of emptiness, has to come from a reasoning process. It is not necessary to go into all these different formalized reasonings as explained, but one has to apply inquiry and first gain an inferential understanding that later can lead to direct experience.

Question: My question is also related to this. Objectively speaking, you said that selflessness exists; but you also said that the form and degree of truth lie in subjectivity. I see a contradiction here in the sense that the subject is still experiencing the self. And secondly, under what condition will the dream-consciousness go outside of reality?

His Holiness: Let's deal with your second question first.

When we are talking of dream consciousness and the dream body, then we are talking about a very different kind of experience. This type of body is autonomous, independent of the physical gross body. We are operating on an entirely different plane.

That dream body can actually see everyday reality. During the day, that dream body of a person can see daytime, and at night see nighttime.

Question: What about prophetic dreams?

His Holiness: That is not unique to the dream body.

The special dream body can depart from this physical body at will. Thus it is something very special.

Some years ago on several occasions I met someone who had experienced that type of power, not due to practice but due to karmic seeds from past lives. The person felt very uncomfortable and asked me what to do. It seemed that during deep sleep he travelled all over the place, witnessing many people and events of the waking world, many of them at a considerable distance away.

As for your question about meditation on emptiness, when we talk about the emptiness of true existence we do not distinguish between object and subject. Both are without true existence. If we search, we can find neither the object perceived nor the perceiving subject, the mind.

Mind can be taken as an object of some other observing consciousness. In this relative context it becomes the object. At that point, when we search for it we will not find it, just as we will not find the subject.

The ultimate reason for negating true existence is that the essence of things is unfindable when you search for it. That is the ultimate sense.

For this reason on the conventional level we have to simply accept things for what they are. Without too much investigation we can accept that this is flower, this is man, this is an Indian, this is a Tibetan, and so forth. We just accept conventional phenomena, and there is no problem at the conventional level. But if we ask further questions, "Who am I? What is the being? What is the self?" from that point of view, we cannot find anything.

Question: And what about consciousness?

His Holiness: Yes, but what is consciousness? We feel consciousness; we have cognition that we call consciousness.

"Today my mind is dull." "Today my mind is clear." We can say that without investigation, without penetration, then the process works.

But when we really search for a subject such as consciousness, we cannot find it.

We can say, "This is my finger, it's very useful." Like this. (A demonstration which arouses laughter.) Nobody argues on that level.

I actually see the colour of my finger, and its shape. But what is 'finger?' Is it colour or the substances of skin, blood, bone? What is finger?

If we analyze particles, the parts of the finger, different substances, we cannot find 'finger.'

The Mind-Only, one of the Buddhist Schools, says that the thing you are looking for does not exist, but that the person who finds that there is nothing exists truly.

Question: Why is Tara related to longevity practice?

His Holiness: Just as Avalokiteshvara is seen as the embodiment of compassion and Manjushri as the embodiment of wisdom, so Tara is seen as the embodiment of subtle energy, or wind.

For the longevity of a person, the continuity of the inner energies is very important.

I think there is a link between these two, because there are some practices for the prolongation of life where one concentrates on the subtle energies.

When I said that Tara practice is good for overcoming illness, I was speaking in the context of the five deities I explained earlier.

For healing meditations in general, a very important tradition is that of the Medicine Buddhas. This is their specific purpose.

When we engage in the practice of visualization of Tara, we imagine a mantra cycle at her heart. Light rays emanate from that circle and dissolve into our body. Then we concentrate with special strength at the points where we have illness. The light rays are hot or cold, depending on the type of illness.

Question: Do these deities symbolize different aspects of Buddha?

His Holiness: Here there are two types of understanding. One way of seeing the situation is that these deities are different aspects of qualities of the Buddhas. The other idea is that the deity symbolizes the method that will lead us to enlightenment, and also symbolizes the enlightenment that we are cultivating. Then when we become enlightened, we become that deity.

In that sense Tara deity, Avalokiteshvara deity or Manjushri deity are different beings from Buddha Shakyamuni. But in another sense they are different aspects of the one Buddha.

Question: Your Holiness told us that the meaning of the word mantra is protection of the mind, that in essence it is positive, creative. But sometimes one hears stories about people with evil intentions, who use mantras to harm others. Is that possible?

His Holiness: The possibility exists. Tantra, or mantra, involves the four types of mystical activities: pacification, increase, power and wrath. It is possible that these could be misused.

There are many types of practitioners. Certainly some are without any deep power of concentration, others are without the altruistic aspiration to highest enlightenment, and still others lack the understanding of emptiness. Some lack all three qualities. It is possible that a few may become corrupt, and through some kind of technique inflict harm.

But that type of power is rather limited.

Question: Should one use the term mantra in that case? It could lose its meaning, its significance.

His Holiness: Such a use of the word would not have the meaning of mantra as protection of the mind.

Mantras are used for many different practices.

There are also many kinds of mantras. For example, there are those expounded by Buddha Vajradhara and written down in the tantric treatises. Then there are certain types of mantras transmitted (to humans) by samsaric deities.

Generally speaking it is very difficult to distinguish between non-Buddhist and Buddhist mantras. Distinction has to be made from the point of view of whether or not there exist the complementary factors of the wisdom which understands emptiness and the altruistic attitude, the aspiration to achieve enlightenment for the benefit of all sentient beings. It is difficult to make that distinction from the mantra itself. One needs to see this from the doctrinal context.

In general it is said that the different forms of deities, mandalas, and mantras based on the theory of a self (*atma*) are from the non-Buddhist tantras. Those deities, mandalas, and mantras essentially based on the theory of selflessness (*anatma*) are from the Buddhist tantras.

Question: Your Holiness, in the Middle Way and their ideas of emptiness, it seems to me that there might lie a danger. The consequence might be the thought, "Well, there is really nothing here anyway, so why should I make any effort for anything!"

His Holiness: As we discussed earlier, first of all we have to distinguish between conventional existence and non-inherent existence. Let's speak about the reasoning of dependent arising. That may give us the answer.

Generally dependent arising indicates some kind of interdependence. To understand that, one has to understand how dependence and independence are directly opposite phenomena, and they exclude the middle. There is nothing that is neither of the two.

Take the example of flower and non-flower, which are direct opposites. Any phenomenon should be either flower or non-flower. There is no third way of existence.

On the other hand, take the examples of flower and table. Although they are mutually exclusive, there are things that are neither of the two. There is a middle.

In the same way, being independent and being dependent are directly opposite. It is very clear that those phenomena which are products of causes depend for their existence on their causes and conditions. In the same way, if it is a whole then it is very obvious that it is dependent on its parts. As long as that phenomenon retains its quality of form, it would always have its directional parts.

Things which have no quality or form, like consciousness, for example, do have parts of different instances, such as earlier and later.

Try and think of a phenomenon that is partless. Physically one can get down to the subatomic level, where there is hardly any possibility of further division of particles. But still there would be directional parts. There is no partlessness.

If there were a particle that did not have directional parts, then how could one say that a composite of such particles could produce a whole? If it were without directional parts, then whatever faced the east should also face the west. There would be no possibility of making composites from such sources.

The writings of the Middle Way School totally negate the theory of partless phenomena. The existence of each phenomenon depends on its own parts.

Another type of dependence is that nothing is findable when we analytically search for its essence. Things depend on their emptiness quality.

If we are contented with mere conventional appearance, then everything is okay. But if we are not satisfied with that mere conventional appearance and instead we search for an essence, some kind of justification from the side of the object, then we do not find anything.

When we finally get to the point where we realize that nothing is findable, the question arises as to whether this indicates that things do not exist at all. But to conclude that nothing exists at all contradicts or own experience, for our experience shows that there is one person who did not find the essence but who nonetheless found the ultimate unfindablility of things.

The valid cognition which perceived the person who was seeking the essence but discovered the unfindability of things would contradict the assertion that things do not exist at all.

Therefore things are there. But when we investigate we cannot find them. They do exist, but only on the basis of imputation. They depend on nominal designation.

No matter in what way we look at things, they always show the characteristics of dependency. They are dependent on casual factors, parts, or on consciousness which gives the designation. These are the three types of dependence.

One must investigate appearances. Ask yourself, "What is the actual nature of that phenomenon, and how does it appear to me?"

Then check whether the way a thing appears and the way it exists correspond. Do they tally or not?

We find that there is a gap between the way things appear and the way they actually exist.

There are two facets to this aspect of the mind.

The first of these is the quality of being a type of mind which for it's arising requires the confirmation of the appearance of true existence. That is to say, it depends for it's arising upon the confirmation of a projected appearance, perhaps influenced by anger or strong attachment. The moment we feel attachment and anger, not only is there appearance but also some kind of confirmation, and we accept that it is one hundred percent positive and feel attached, or one hundred per cent negative and feel repelled.

If we see an enemy who is a hundred per cent enemy, then he should be everybody's enemy. But my enemy might be the best friend of others.

The enemy is not a hundred percent negative. This was only an exaggeration produced as a result of a feeling of strong dislike. All negative thought must have that kind of confirmation. Positive thought does not.

Emptiness is not a subject that someone with knowledge can explain and someone else will immediately understand. It is not like pointing to a car and the other person sees and understands.

Here knowledge of the subject and one's own inner experience must grow together.

Thus time is also involved. You cannot gain the inner experience within days or weeks. It can take even years of concentration and experimentation. Gradually, however, the matter becomes more and more clear.

Appendix

A Tantric Meditation Simplified for Beginners

by
Tenzin Gyatso, the Fourteenth Dalai Lama

Preparing for the Sessions

The meditation should be performed in a quiet, pleasant place, or in a part of your dwelling that is appropriate. Begin by mindfully sweeping and cleaning the area of practice.

Upon the table to be used as the altar you should arrange an image or statue of the Buddha, as well as of the three Bodhisattvas symbolizing the three essential Buddha-attributes: Avalokitesvara(compassion), Manjusri (wisdom), and Vajrapani (energy or right action): and also Arya Tara, who symbolizes the activity of all the Buddhas. In this manner Buddha Form is represented.

In addition, to the right of the assembly place a copy of a sacred scripture, preferably one of the *Prajnaparamita Sutras*, to symbolize Buddha Speech.

Finally, to the left of the assembly place a miniature stupa (reliquary monument), to symbolize Buddha Mind.

If a text of the *Prajnaparamita* is not available, any Buddhist sutra can be substituted. Similarly, if the images or statues are difficult to obtain, just a statue of the Buddha will suffice.

Even that is not indispensable. The one absolute essential is a proper state of mind.

Next one sets forth offerings. These should consist of pure water, flowers, incense, light, food and sound. They should be set out as elegantly as possible to denote heartfelt respect and appreciation.

When all has been prepared, seat yourself cross-legged upon a cushion, facing east, in the vajra posture (both feet folded into your lap, with the soles facing upward) or the half-vajra posture (one foot up and the other drawn under the body). If both of these are too difficult, try to adopt one of them for a little while and then sit in whatever position is comfortable.

The Preliminary Meditations

Now reflect: "Our bodily actions are good, bad or indifferent in accordance with our state of mind. Therefore mind-training comes before all else. Now that we enjoy the good fortune of being in the human state and are accordingly endowed with greater powers of thought and achievement than other beings, how sad it is that we should spend our lives striving merely for happiness in this life.

If striving thus were really productive of permanent happiness, then among the many people in this world endowed with power, wealth and friendship, there would surely be some blessed with a large measure of real and lasting happiness. But in truth, though there are indeed relative differences in the amount and intensity of happiness enjoyed, every single one of us be he a ruler or warrior, be he rich, middle class or poor is subject to all sorts of physical and mental suffering, especially torments of the mind."

Carry this reflection further by seeking within yourself the causes of suffering and happiness.

As you come to know the nature of these causes more fully, you will recognize the mind is the ultimate cause of suffering and that there are also subsidiary factors that either augment or decrease the impurities of mind. These impurities can be removed; and once the mind has become stabilized it can be transformed into an enlightened mind as skill in dealing with the hindrances increases.

Contemplate like this for some time, and gradually generate the sense that it is so.

It is vitally important to eliminate the cause of suffering and to acquire the cause of happiness.

However, to attain any kind of lasting happiness we must diligently accumulate its causes and to eliminate suffering we must use appropriate means to prevent the arising of its causes.

These two purposes can be accomplished only by full recognition of the true causes of joy and sorrow.

To accomplish these two purposes, it is useful to rely upon and show the utmost confidence in the Buddhadharma, a confidence that gains its strength from the most probing analysis undertaken in the light of inquiry and reason.

Taking Refuge

Then mentally recite these words:

> I go for refuge to the Buddhas, the Fully Enlightened Ones, who guide beings by expounding to them the pure, true teachings of the Dharma, which is the fruit of the supreme wisdom derived from their direct experience.
>
> I go for refuge to the Dharma, which affords full transcendence of all suffering and leads to true happiness; for the Dharma connotes the elimination of all negativity and the fulfillment of all creative qualities as a result of wholesome thought and action functioning through body, speech and mind.
>
> I go for refuge to the Sangha, the supreme community, whose feet are firmly set on the path to enlightenment. Upon them I place my unswerving reliance for that spiritual assistance of which I stand in need.

The Visualization

In the space before your forehead visualize a resplendent throne. Upon it sits Buddha Shakyamuni, his legs crossed in the vajra posture.

His right hand is in the gesture of calling the earth as witness. Thus it points downward, with the tips of the fingers touching the seat of the throne.

His left hand holds a bowl full of the nectars of wisdom, the palm at the level of his naval.

Buddha Shakyamuni is visualized as being slightly larger than other members of the sacred assembly. He shines with a golden radiance.

To either side of the throne and a little to the front stand Shariputra and Maudgalyayana, Buddha's two chief disciples, each holding in his right hand a metal staff and in his left a bowl.

The Buddha and both of these disciples are dressed as monks. To the right of the Buddha is Avalokiteshvara, his body white in colour. He is seated upon a lotus throne, hands joined palm to palm at the heart.

To the left, also upon a lotus throne, is Manjushri, his body golden in colour. He holds a sword of wisdom in his right hand, and a sacred text in his left.

Seated upon a lotus cushion in front of the Buddha is Vajrapani, dark-blue in colour, holding a vajra in his right hand and, with his left, showing the threatening gesture.

Behind the Buddha, also seated upon a lotus cushion, sits Arya Tara, emerald-green in colour. Her right hand is in the gesture of giving blessings, and her left hand holds a blue lotus as she reveals the gesture of giving refuge.

All four of these Bodhisattva figures are seated on lotus thrones. They all wear beautiful silken garments and jewelled ornaments. Their bodies are radiant with light and life.

To the right of this holy assembly is a mound of sacred texts containing the essence of the teachings symbolizing the true path to enlightenment and the true cessation of suffering.

To the left of the assembly is a glorious stupa to symbolize the supreme wisdom of all Buddhas.

You should regard the visualized assembly to be of the true essence of all refuge objects.

Now visualize your father and male relatives, including those who have previously passed away, as being seated to your right. Your mother and all female relatives are seated to your left. Your enemies are seated in front of you, and those who esteem you are seated behind you.

Surrounding them are all the beings in the universe. These are visualized as appearing in human form.

In your mind you see this great concourse of humanity joining with you in reciting with rapt concentration the words of refuge.

One contemplates the virtues of the supreme body, speech and mind of the visualized assembly, and light-rays issue forth from them. It falls upon the entire concourse of living beings, both you and those around you.

You should imagine that this light purifies you and all others of every spiritual stain and obscuration.

Then with heartfelt attention recite these words twenty-one times, or as much as possible: *Namo Buddhaya, Namo Dharmaya, Namo Sanghaya.*

Thereafter, turn your mind to the beings around you, who are exactly like you. They want lasting happiness but continually neglect to bring about its cause; they long to be spared their ever-present suffering but fail to abandon its cause.

Understand clearly that suffering will never cease until its cause has been erased. Far from decreasing, it will remain with you forever until you abandon its cause.

The way to eliminate the cause of suffering is not easy to discover. However, already you have begun to go a little way forward by investigating what to hold on to and what to let go.

You must practise assiduously and progress in skill until you discover the whole of that transcendence and growth, something essential to the happiness and comfort of the living beings, whom you have learned to universally cherish.

With these waves of thought in the ocean of your mind, chant the following verse.

> To the Buddhas, the Dharma and the Supreme Community
> I turn for refuge until enlightenment is gained.

By the strength of my practices, such as the six perfections,
May enlightenment be attained for the benefit of all.

Next concentrate on the refuge objects visualized before you. Offer the seven-limbed prayer in their imagined presence. These seven limbs are as follows.

The first is that of prostration. Here one recollects the objects of refuge and pays homage to them. One can either offer a full prostration to them, touching the ground with arms, forehead and fully extended body; or a half prostration, touching the ground with forehead, elbows, knees and toes; or simply place your palms together and intone the following verse, keeping the mind in the sphere of concentrated veneration.

To the Enlightened Beings of the three times,
And to the Dharma and the Supreme Community
I reverently pay heartfelt homage
With a spirit infused with joy.

The second limb is that of making offerings. We visualize offering all material things, together with all the pure and naturally beautiful phenomena of the world. We take these into our mind and offer them to the visualized assembly, in conjunction with the following words.

Just as Manjushri and the other Bodhisattvas
Made countless offerings to all the Buddhas,
So do I now make offerings
To the Buddhas and host of Bodhisattvas.

The third limb is that of acknowledging our shortcomings and failures, both those of this life and those of all previous lives.

Reflect upon the cause of our sufferings, which is negative karma and delusion. Of these, delusion is the greater foe, for it is the delusions that activate our negative karma. Thus they bring misery to every living being.

These delusions, the mental defilements that wreak the most fearful harm, are the true enemy of all living beings.

Having remained constantly under the power of this great enemy for so long, we have surely stored up a formidable supply of negative karmic instincts that, unless we take remedial measures, will bear us a bitter fruit indeed; for our karmic seeds cannot fade away or decline of their own accord.

Now is the time, here in the presence of the refuge objects, to acknowledge our failings of this and previous lives, and to regret them. We should resolve that henceforth, even in dreams, we shall commit no more of them.

Reflecting in this way, repeat the following verse.

> Throughout the beginningless time of samsara
> In this and all previous lifetimes
> I have collected countless negative karmas
> Through my wrong understanding and folly,
> Often even rejoicing in my errors
> And woefully enslaved by ignorance.
> I acknowledge all this wrongdoing
> And bow before you in humility.

The limb of rejoicing is next. One rejoices in the goodness and merit of oneself and all others.

The cause of happiness is goodness, which as well as conferring immediate benefits, also produces forces that will lead to great benefits in the distant future. Fully rejoice in the vast reservoir of meritorious energy shared by you and all others. Meritorious energy is the best friend and true protector of all beings.

Reflecting in that way you should recite the following words.

> In that supreme mind which shines on all beings,
> Bringing aid and benefit to every sentient being,
> I profoundly rejoice with the utmost veneration.
> I rejoice in the thought of enlightenment, and in the
> Dharma,
> That ocean of happiness for every sentient being
> Wherein abides the welfare of all that lives.

The fifth limb is the prayer that the great masters turn the Wheel of the Dharma.

One implores all the enlightened masters who have attained to perfect knowledge of spiritual practice to turn the Wheel of the Dharma for the benefit of all beings. This request is made with the following verse.

> With hands folded in salutation
> I entreat the Buddhas of the ten directions
> To cause the lamp of the Dharma to shine brightly
> For all those wandering amidst suffering wrought by delusion.

Next is the limb of requesting the masters not to pass away, but to remain in the world and work for the evolution of the living beings.

One entreats the Buddhas not to enter final nirvana, but to remain forever to guide and protect all sentient beings. This is done in accordance with the following verse.

> With hands folded in salutation
> I implore all Buddhas thinking to enter parinirvana
> To remain in the world for ages without end,
> So that life will not become lost to darkness.

The seventh limb is that of the dedication of merits.

Here by means of the following verse one requests that the merit of performing this practice, and also any meritorious energy of yourself and all other beings, may be turned to the aspiration that all living beings may attain happiness and perfect enlightenment.

> May any meritorious energy generated
> By my engaging in this spiritual practice
> Be dedicated to the enlightenment of all beings
> And may they be made happy in every way.

The Mantra Recitation

Concentrate for a while on Buddha and the visualized assembly.

When you have a clear picture of them in your mind, visualize a flat luminous disc in the centre of the chest of each. In each disc is a symbolic syllable, or mantric seed sound, as follows: *Mum* for the Buddha; *Hrih* for Avalokitesvara; *Dhih* for Manjushri; *Hum* for Vajrapani; and *Tam* for Tara.

Each of these symbolic syllables is surrounded by a mantra. Thus there are five mantras. At this point in the meditation you should recite each of them seven, twenty-one, a hundred-and-eight, or as many times as possible.

The mantras are as follows:

> *Om muni muni maha muni ye svaha*–the mantra of Buddha;
> *Om mani padme hum*–that of Avalokiteshvara;
> *Om wagi shvari mum*–that of Manjushri;
> *Om vajra pani hum*–that of Vajrapani;
> *Om tara tuttare ture svaha*–that of Tara.

Then to symbolize that all the outer deceptive phenomena are the same in their nature of emptiness, you visualize as follows.

Avalokitesvara slowly dissolves into light and vanishes into the Buddha's head. Manjushri dissolves into light and then into the Buddha's neck. Vajrapani dissolves into his chest, Tara into his navel, and the two chief disciples into the two sides of his body.

Thereafter you should retain a clear visualization only of the Buddha. Concentrate as long as you can in this way.

Om muni muni māhamuniye svāhā   MUM

Om mani padme hūm   HRĪH

Om wagi shvari mum   DHIH

Om vajrapāni hūm   HŪM

Om tare ture tuttare ture svāhā   TĀM

After that the Buddha also changes slowly into pure light, beginning from the top and the bottom, and vanishing into the luminous disc at the centre of his heart. The disc dissolves into the mantra. It in turn dissolves into the symbolic syllable it surrounds.

The symbolic syllable then changes into light, and only a dot at the top is left. That also slowly vanishes, until merely the formless clear light remains.

Fix your mind for some moments in meditation upon the emptiness nature of all appearance. Next, to symbolize all the relatively existing pleasures that spring forth and become manifest, though they are the same in their very essence as voidness itself, you should visualize that the entire assembly reappears as before, in the space in front of you.

Close the meditation session in a spirit of enthusiasm and joy.

As you rise from your meditation cushion and go about the various activities of the day, carry the vision of Buddha and the assembly with you at all times. Merge it in with your every activity.

When you take your meals, offer a small portion to the Buddhas and Bodhisattvas as a means of reminding yourself of the spiritual path.

Then at night as you go to sleep you can visualize that your head lies peacefully in the lap of the Buddha.

Thus with all deeds and at all times you should attempt to keep the Buddha for your witness and use your body, speech and mind always in creative, positive ways.

If you practise this meditation once a day, twice a day (morning and evening), or four times (morning, afternoon, evening and night) you should begin with short sessions and then gradually build them in length, increasing the time as your maturity in concentration and attention grows. If you practice in this way, there is no doubt that many beneficial effects will arise.

Sarva Mangalam !

Text Quoted by His Holiness

Indian Texts:-

The Avatamsaka Sutra
Tib. *Phal-po-chei-mdo*
Skt. *Buddhaavatamsaka-sutra*

Fundamental Treatise of Wisdom
Tib. *rTsa-baishes-rab*
Skt. *Mula-madhyamaka-karika-shastra*

A Guide to the Bodhisattva Ways
Tib. *Byang-chub-sems-dpai-spyod-pa-la-'jug-pa*
Skt. *Bodhisattva-charya-avatara*

The Perfection of Wisdom Sutra
Tib. *Phar-phyin-gyi-mdo*
Skt. *Prajnaparamita-sutra*

The Sutra on Monastic Discipline
Tib. *'Dul-baimdo*
Skt. *Vinayasutra*

A Treasury of Abhidharma
Tib. *Chos-mngon-par-mdzod*
Skt. *Abhidharmakosha*

Sutra Unravelling the Thought of Buddha
Tib. *mDo-sde-dgongs-'grel*
Skt. *Samdhinirmochanasutra*

Tibetan Texts:-

Eight Verses for Training the Mind
Tib. *bLo-sbyong-tshigs-brgyad-ma*

A Tantric Meditation Simplified for Beginners
Tib. *Sangs-rgyas-byang-sems-sgom-tshul*